UNI

UNIVERSE CARDS

PERSONAL PREDICTIONS FOR THE 21ST CENTURY

Kay Stopforth

We must not forget that the human soul,
however independently created
our philosophy represents it as being,
is inseparable
in its birth and in its growth
from the Universe into which it is born.
Pierre Teilhard de Chardin

Thorsons

Thorsons
An Imprint of HarperCollins*Publishers*
77–85 Fulham Palace Road
Hammersmith, London W6 8JB

The Thorsons website address is:
www.thorsons.com

Published by Thorsons 1999

1 3 5 7 9 10 8 6 4 2

© Kay Stopforth 1999

Kay Stopforth asserts the moral right to
be identified as the author of this work

A catalogue record for this book
is available from the British Library

ISBN 0 7225 3957 6

Printed in Great Britain by
Woolnough Bookbinding Ltd, Irthlingborough

All rights reserved. No part of this publication may be reproduced, stored in a retrieval system, or transmitted, in any form or by any means, electronic, mechanical, photocopying, recording or otherwise, without the prior permission of the publishers.

CONTENTS

Acknowledgements vii
Introduction .xi
About the Universe Cards xi
About the Hubble Space Telescope xii
The Universe as Mirror xiii
How to Use the Cards 1
Preparing to Use the Cards 2
Asking a Question 3
Interpreting the Cards 4
Journeying With the Cards 5
The Four Forces Cards 7
Caring For Your Cards 8

THE UNIVERSE CARDS 11

Earth 13
Asteroid 17
Satellite 21
Solar System .25
Comet 29
Star 32
Binary System 35
Star Cluster 39
Red Dwarf 43
Brown Dwarf 46
Red Giant 49

White Dwarf	52
Black Dwarf	55
Nova	58
Supernova	62
Neutron Star	65
Pulsar	69
Nebula: Star Birth	72
Nebula: Star Death	76
Planet Formation	80
Galaxy Formation	83
Spiral Galaxy	87
Active Galaxy	90
Elliptical Galaxy	93
Quasar	97
Black Hole	100
Galaxy Collision	104
Galaxy Cluster	108
Distant Galaxies	112
Dark Matter	115
The Universe	118
The Four Forces: Gravity	121
The Four Forces: Electromagnetism	125
The Four Forces: The Strong Force	129
The Four Forces: The Weak Force	132

ACKNOWLEDGEMENTS

Many friends have assisted at the birth of the Universe Cards and I send my love and gratitude to them all. Present at the conception was Robert Neufeld, who provided the original inspiration. The following people gave moral, practical and spiritual support during the exciting and sometimes challenging process of gestation: Terry Bowrage, Steve Gray, Alison Lees, Chris Morton, Ceri Thomas and Natalie Tobert. Annie Spencer and my fellow Shamankas gave me a boost at just the right time with their positive feedback and willingness to act as 'guinea pigs'. Belinda Budge at Thorsons believed in the cards enough to facilitate their birth into the world. Finally, and most of all, Keith Bonnick, without whom I would never have got started — my love always.

PICTURE CREDITS AND ACKNOWLEDGEMENTS

Material created with support to AURA/STScI from NASA contract NAS5-26555 is reproduced here with permission.
Earth: Earth from Apollo 17: Courtesy of National Space Science Data Center, World Data Center-A for Rockets and Satellites, The Principal Investigator, Dr. Frederick J. Doyle.
Asteroid: The asteroid Gaspra: Courtesy of National Space Science Data Center, World Data Center-A for Rockets and Satellites, The Team Leader, Dr. Michael J.S. Belton, The Galileo Project.

UNIVERSE CARDS

Satellite: Montage of Jupiter and the Galilean satellites: Courtesy of National Space Science Data Center, World Data Center-A for Rockets and Satellites, The Team Leader, Dr. Bradford A. Smith.

Solar System : Montage of Saturn and several of its satellites: Courtesy of National Space Science Data Center, World Data Center-A for Rockets and Satellites, The Team Leader, Dr. Bradford A. Smith.

Comet: Comet Hyakutake: Courtesy of H. A. Weaver (Advanced Research Corp.), HST Comet Hyakutake Observing Team and NASA.

Star: The Horsehead Nebula, IC 434 and NGC 2024 in Orion: Copyright Anglo-Australian Observatory/Royal Observatory Edinburgh. Photograph made from UK Schmidt plates by David Malin.

Binary System: Copyright John Foster/Science Photo Library.

Star Cluster: M45, The Pleiades and their reflection nebulae: Copyright Anglo-Australian Observatory/Royal Observatory Edinburgh. Photograph made from UK Schmidt plates by David Malin.

Red Dwarf: Original artwork. Copyright Mark A. Garlick.

Brown Dwarf: Original artwork. Copyright Mark A. Garlick.

Red Giant: Antares and the Rho Ophiuchi Dark Cloud: Copyright Anglo-Australian Observatory/Royal Observatory Edinburgh. Photograph made from UK Schmidt plates by David Malin.

White Dwarf: Original artwork. Copyright Mark A. Garlick.

Black Dwarf: Original artwork. Copyright Mark A. Garlick.

Nova: Eta Carinae: Courtesy of J. Morse (University of Colorado) and NASA.

Supernova: Vela Supernova remnant: Copyright Anglo-Australian Observatory. Photograph by David Malin.

ACKNOWLEDGEMENTS

Neutron Star: Crab Nebula: Courtesy of J. Hester and P. Scowen (Arizona State University) and NASA.

Pulsar: Copyright Julian Baum/New Scientist/Science Photo Library.

Star Birth: Lagoon Nebula detail: Courtesy of A. Caulet (ST-ECF, ESA) and NASA.

Star Death: Hourglass Nebula MyCn18: Courtesy of R. Sahai and J. Trauger (JPL), the WFPC2 Science Team and NASA.

Planet Formation: Close-up of 'proplyds' in Orion: Courtesy of C.R. O'Dell/Rice University and NASA.

Galaxy Formation: Hubble deep field in infrared: Courtesy of R. Thompson (University of Arizona) and NASA.

Spiral Galaxy: M100 galactic nucleus: Courtesy of STScI, AURA and NASA.

Active Galaxy: Radio galaxy NGC 5128 (Centaurus A): Copyright Anglo-Australian Observatory. Photograph by David Malin.

Elliptical Galaxy: Elliptical galaxy M87 (NGC 4486): Copyright Anglo-Australian Observatory. Photograph by David Malin.

Quasar: HST's 100.000th Observation, a distant Quasar: Courtesy of C. Steidel (CalTech) and NASA.

Black Hole: Active galaxy Centaurus A: Courtesy of E. Schreier (STScI) and NASA.

Galaxy Collision: Colliding galaxies NGC 4038 and NGC 4039: Courtesy of B. Whitmore (STScI) and NASA.

Galaxy Cluster: Cartwheel Galaxy: Courtesy of K. Borne (STScI) and NASA.

Distant Galaxies: Gravitational lens galaxy cluster 0024+1654: Courtesy of W.N. Colley and E. Turner (Princeton University), J.A. Tyson (Bell Labs, Lucent Technologies) and NASA.

Dark Matter: Infrared Hubble Deep Field South: Courtesy of R. Williams (STScI), the HDF-South team and NASA.

UNIVERSE CARDS

The Universe Astronomers discover an infrared background glow in the universe: Courtesy of M. Hauser (STScI), the COBE/DIRBE Science Team and NASA.

The 4 Forces: Gravity: M16 Starbirth Clouds: Courtesy of J. Hester and P. Scowen (Arizona State University) and NASA.

The 4 Forces: Electromagnetism: Cygnus Loop: Courtesy of J. Hester (Arizona State University) and NASA.

The 4 Forces: The Strong Force: Nebula M1-67: Courtesy of Y. Grosdidier (University of Montreal and Observatoire de Strasbourg), A. Moffat (University of Montreal), G. Joncas (Universite Laval), A. Acker (Observatoire de Strasbourg) and NASA.

The 4 Forces: The Weak Force: Ring Nebula: Courtesy of Hubble Heritage Team (AURA/STScI/NASA).

INTRODUCTION

ABOUT THE UNIVERSE CARDS

The Universe Cards act as a mirror for our inner selves, with the natural phenomena of the universe reflecting our own natures and our own destinies. The cards form a symbolic journey from the Earth out into space, exploring the mysteries of the universe. This outward journey is mirrored by an inner one of self-discovery, an exploration of our own mysteries and dark places. Although the cards do not map a literal astronomical course, they generally move outwards, embracing ever larger phenomena. Each card takes us further out into the universe, past stars, nebulae and galaxies, ending with the Universe Card itself.

There are 35 Universe Cards in all, starting with the Earth Card. The meaning of each card is closely tied to the nature of the phenomenon it describes. For example, the Supernova Card describes a time of sudden crisis, challenge or dramatic change, which is related to the dramatic, explosive nature of a real supernova. The text for each Universe Card is divided into four parts. The card is described by a single keyword, then a brief outline of the scientific background is given, followed by a full interpretation of the card's symbolic meaning. Lastly, a suggested activity — usually a ritual or a visualization — is given to deepen the understanding of the card. There are also four special cards in the pack, known as the Four Forces Cards. These cards represent the four fundamental forces known in the universe: gravity, electromagnetism, the strong force and the weak force. See 'About the Four Forces Cards' (page 7) for more information about these cards.

About the Hubble Space Telescope

Many of the cards use images from the Hubble Space Telescope. These images, available to the world through the internet, have thrilled and inspired many. In the last few years, the Hubble Space Telescope has radically expanded our view of the universe. Without the Earth's atmosphere to block and distort the images, Hubble can look further and deeper than has ever been possible. Phenomena such as Black Holes and Quasars, which were objects of theoretical conjecture, have now been found and documented by Hubble. Our understanding of the origins of the universe has also been enhanced by Hubble's ability to look deeper into space, and consequently further back in time. The incredibly distant objects photographed by the telescope are so far away that the light that is now reaching us from these objects is millions or billions of years old. We are seeing these objects as they were in the early years of the universe. Thus Hubble enables us simultaneously to perceive over unimaginable distances and to look back over unimaginable periods of time.

The Universe as Mirror

Throughout history, our mythology has provided us with a mirror of ourselves as people. Our stories and legends have helped define us and helped us to understand ourselves. Most human mythologies have also encompassed our physical world in some way. The sun, moon and stars have been both directly worshipped and symbolically represented as deities. Indeed, most early civilizations, and many indigenous cultures today, see the divine in everything around them. They not only worship the heavens, but believe that every tree, every rock is a living thing with a living spirit. Dare we imagine that the universe too could be alive? Could the universe be a living, self-regulating entity with a spirit, if not a consciousness, that we can encompass? Could it, like the symbolic representation of the sun, moon and stars in astrology and the tarot, be a symbol and a mirror for us? Maybe by expanding our awareness to embrace the universe we can also expand our sense of ourselves as people and move closer to expressing the entirety of ourselves.

HOW TO USE THE CARDS

As you are about to consult the Universe Cards, it is important to bear a few things in mind. The cards are a kind of oracle. They answer questions and provide insight into inner motivations and outer events. They are not a way of foreseeing the future and they will not give you winning lottery numbers or racing tips! If you approach the cards with this kind of aim in mind, you will generally be given short shrift. Remember, the cards are a mirror — the nature of your intention in using them will be reflected back to you. If you approach the cards with openness and integrity, you will be repaid in kind. Unlike most divination packs, there are no set spreads with the Universe Cards. The cards are designed to be completely open to the intuition of the user. However, there are some guidelines for preparation and use of the cards.

PREPARING TO USE THE CARDS

It is important to consult the cards in a quiet, peaceful environment where you will be undisturbed by the noise and activity of everyday life. It is also necessary to quieten the mind before attempting to use the cards. If you practise meditation, yoga or any other method of concentration or relaxation, now would be a good time to employ it. Otherwise, simply take a few minutes to sit in silence with the cards in front of you. If music helps, then listen to a favourite piece of music while you do this. The ideal state of mind you are looking for is relaxed yet focused. After you have relaxed and quietened down by your chosen method for about ten minutes, pick up the cards. Continue with your relaxation while you slowly handle and shuffle the cards. You can use any method for shuffling the cards, but ensure they are thoroughly mixed. If you have a question to ask, focus on this question as you continue shuffling. Imagine that you are charging the cards with the energy of your question as you handle them. If you do not have a specific question, but are looking for more general guidance, such as a guiding card for a particular day or month or occasion, similarly concentrate on charging the cards with this intention.

HOW TO USE THE CARDS

ASKING A QUESTION

Continue handling the cards for about five minutes and when you feel ready, spread out all the cards on the floor or on a table, making sure they are all face down. Now simply pick a card or cards to answer your question. Choose the cards quickly, without too much reflection or dithering. Put yourself in the hands of your unconscious and let your hand guide you. Try not to think about what you are doing. It is up to you how many cards you pick, let your intuition guide you. As a general rule, if you are asking a straightforward question, pick one card. If you are asking a question where there are two or more alternatives, pick a separate card for each alternative. Keep in mind which option applies to which card as you are choosing them. In general, choose one card to cover each aspect of a question. For example, if your initial question is, 'What would be the consequences of continuing in my job or starting to work for myself?', divide the question into two. Pick one card for 'What would be the consequences of continuing in my job?' and another card for 'What would be the consequences of starting to work for myself?'. Avoid 'Should I…?' questions, such as 'Should I leave my job?'. Use the format 'What would happen if…?' or 'What would be the consequences if…?'. The phrasing of your question is important, because as a rule, the clearer and more specific your question, the clearer the answer will be from the cards. For this reason, it is often useful to read the cards with a friend, who may be able to help you refine and focus your question.

INTERPRETING THE CARDS

When you have chosen your card or cards, turn them over and spend a few seconds looking at the images on the cards before you turn to the interpretation. What is your initial reaction to the images? Do you like them? Do they make you feel uncomfortable? Record your initial gut reaction to the images before you look at the interpretation for the card.

The interpretation for each card is divided into four parts; *keyword*, *background*, *interpretation* and *activity*. The *keyword* is a single word which sums up the essence of a card's meaning. The *background* section gives the astronomical explanation of the card. This section is important, as the meaning of the card is inextricably bound to the nature of the phenomenon itself. The *interpretation* section outlines the symbolic meaning of the card and the *activity* section suggests a ritual or visualization which will help you to deepen your understanding of the card. Although you may not particularly want to commit yourself to the suggested activity, I would recommend that you at least try it — and be honest with yourself about why you may not want to do it! Many of the suggested activities are powerful rituals which will work at a much deeper level than the conscious mind. Simply reading the interpretation of the card is a first step. The activities are intended to activate the healing or knowing processes symbolized by each card. If you draw more than one card and are unsure about which activity to choose, again let your intuition guide you. If you wish to choose only one activity, consider each card and then, as a general rule, choose the activity you feel least comfortable with! If you really cannot decide, then try them all. Some of the activities require more commitment than others in terms of time. If you have chosen one that involves a longer commitment, then try it for a short time. You can always abandon it if it does not feel right for you. There is no such thing as failure here. These activities are meant to assist you, not to make you feel inadequate or guilty. If one of the activities stands out for you and has a particular resonance, then go with it. This sense of resonance is the voice of your intuition and intuition should not be ignored.

JOURNEYING WITH THE CARDS

You may also want to use the concept of the journey. If you cannot describe your predicament in a single question, imagine it as a journey and choose a card to represent each stage of the journey. You may not consciously know what these stages actually are or where your journey is going, but just go with the flow. You may tend to choose more cards than if you were asking a specific question. Simply begin choosing cards and continue until you feel your journey is complete. Place the cards in a line face down in the order in which you have chosen them. Consider each card in order. The first card you chose is the starting point for your journey and it usually describes where you are here and now. The final card describes a possible outcome or destination for your journey. The cards in between describe how you get there. As you consider the meaning of each card, think of how it connects with the meaning of the cards before and after. What is the story being mapped out here? Interpreting this journey may require considerable thought and reflection, but it can also be highly insightful and not a little surprising. If you are unsure which activity or activities to choose from the journey cards, a good rule of thumb is to choose the activities from the first and last cards of the journey. But, as with everything in the Universe Cards, it is really up to you.

How to Use the Cards

The Four Forces Cards

An infinite variety of events is taking place in the universe at any given time, from the creation and destruction of stars to the comparatively mundane activities of the planets in our solar system. However, this vast array of activity is made possible by only four different types of catalyst. These catalysts are known as forces and there are four forces that exist in our universe. These are gravity, electromagnetism, the strong force and the weak force. Gravity, which is probably the most familiar to us, acts as a kind of glue to hold the universe together. Electromagnetism is responsible for light, radio waves and other forms of radiation. The strong and weak forces operate only within the nuclei of atoms, but are nevertheless essential to the existence of our universe. It is now believed that all forces are actually facets of a single superforce that was created by the Big Bang.

The Four Forces Cards are different from the other cards in the pack. They are not part of the journey outwards into the universe symbolized by the other cards. Yet at the same time they permeate each stage of the journey. The Four Forces Cards represent inner processes which are timeless. Whereas the other cards represent our reactions to external events, the Forces Cards focus exclusively on our inner world. Although other cards may describe inner processes, these are usually triggered by external events. There is always an interaction with the world implied, a sense that the meaning described has its place in our journey through life, through this world. The Four Forces Cards deal with inner processes that recur repeatedly in our lives and are not necessarily triggered by outer events. These cards describe eternal themes that are always present in our lives. Drawing one of the Four Forces Cards is an important signal that you are particularly connected to the timeless and eternal at this moment. If one of these cards appears in a reading, the implications of your inquiry are wider than the current situation. This may be part of a repeating pattern in your life and the real issue at stake is something deeper than the current situation may indicate.

CARING FOR YOUR CARDS

Consider your pack of Universe Cards as a living entity. As you use the cards, they will become charged with your energy, becoming increasingly 'alive'. It is a good idea to wrap them in a special piece of fabric to protect them both physically and energetically. Traditionally, tarot cards are wrapped in silk, but you can use any material that feels right. Always turn the card at the bottom of the pack inwards so that the face of the card is towards the rest of the pack. This helps to keep in the energy you have put into the cards through handling them. Having the face of a card showing at the bottom of the pack is like leaving a door open or leaving the top off a container. It allows energy to drain away. If you have a special or sacred space such as an altar, it is a good idea to keep the cards there. Alternatively, store them in a safe place and try to keep them in the same place all the time. Do not leave them lying around or allow the pack to become split up. If you have young children, a safe, inaccessible storage place is a must! Treat your cards as if they were an honoured guest in your house — you want them to feel safe and looked after.

THE UNIVERSE CARDS

EARTH
Keyword: Source

BACKGROUND: A growing understanding of our home planet has been the first step in understanding the universe. For much of history, humanity has believed the Earth to be flat, although some ancient civilizations guessed the truth and made accurate estimates of the Earth's circumference. When it was finally accepted that the Earth was round, it was still believed that the sun, planets and stars were all embedded in a crystalline 'celestial sphere' around the Earth. It was not until the 16th century that the Polish scholar Copernicus suggested that the Earth and all the planets might revolve around the sun. Today we have a much more detailed understanding of how the Earth works and we can make very accurate measurements of its size and behaviour using satellite technology. Although the Earth is now familiar to us, there are still many mysteries to be contemplated. For example, biologist James Lovelock has theorized that the Earth as a whole is a living system, a self-regulating entity called Gaia that literally has a life of its own.

INTERPRETATION: Every journey has its beginning somewhere, its point of origin. The starting point for humanity is always Earth. Our journey through the universe begins and ends with Earth, our precious, life-giving home. There are many wonders in the universe but there is nothing quite so beautiful or unique as our home planet. If you draw the Earth Card, you are being asked to examine, literally, where you are coming from. What is your point of origin? This may be the town in which you grew up, your family, your ancestors. Determine what has made you who you are, the very source of your being. Look within at who you are fundamentally, without the 'masks' you wear for others. Are you in tune with this essential level of your being? Or have you become disconnected from your source? We can often lose touch with who we truly are. Other considerations such as duty, the need to earn a living or care for others may be dominant in our lives. We may feel that life lacks meaning, although all our material needs are met. Any of these things may indicate that we have lost touch with our source. The Earth Card may be telling you that it is time to look within for answers. It is easy to become distracted through the pressures of daily life, work, relationships, family, etc. The Earth Card indicates that you need to take some time for yourself. You need quiet time for self-examination, to begin to make the journey within. It may at first seem difficult to justify making time for something as intangible as self-examination and we also may avoid it because it makes us feel uncomfortable. However, if we continue to ignore the call of the Earth Card, we are ultimately cheating ourselves of our own birthright — to express freely the essence of ourselves.

ACTIVITY: ASKING THE EARTH FOR A SYMBOL
Sit quietly in a room in which you feel comfortable. Make sure that the door is closed and that you will be undisturbed. Sit or lie down, close your eyes and take a few minutes to relax. Imagine that you are floating in space above the Earth. Feel what it is like to look down upon your home planet, to see the Earth in its entirety. Now ask the Earth to give you a symbolic object to represent your source. Imagine that the object is slowly floating up towards you from the Earth, gradually coming into focus as it gets closer and closer. When the object reaches you examine it closely and hold it in your hands. What does it feel like? What is it for? Try not to let your rational mind interfere or judge if the object seems strange or inexplicable. If you are puzzled by the object, ask the Earth a question about it. Ask for an explanation of its meaning. Once you have asked all the questions you want, return to the room. Make a drawing of your object and write down your experiences and any answers to questions. Keep the drawing in a prominent place and keep

looking at it, reflecting upon it. The object's true meaning will probably reveal itself to you only gradually. Remember, this object symbolizes your source, the essence of who you are.

ASTEROID
Keyword: (In)dependence

BACKGROUND: An asteroid is a lump of rock that can vary in size from a few feet to several kilometres across. The asteroids in our Solar System are mostly grouped together in orbit between Mars and Jupiter. This group is known as the asteroid belt. The largest asteroid in the belt is called Ceres and is about 1,000km in diameter. Many of the other asteroids have also been recorded, photographed and given poetic names such as Pallas or Vesta. However, nobody knows exactly how many asteroids exist as most are too small to be seen from Earth. It is possible that the asteroids are a remnant of a planet that was somehow destroyed earlier in the evolution of the Solar System.

INTERPRETATION: Each asteroid in the asteroid belt is an independent entity, some with individual names, yet each one shares the same orbit around the sun. The asteroids are simultaneously interdependent and separate. This polarity between attachment and freedom is the essence of the Asteroid Card. We all need people in our lives, we all need a certain amount of stability, but we also need spontaneity and independence. If the Asteroid Card appears in a reading, it indicates that the dialectic between dependence and independence is being particularly activated in you. You may be feeling frustrated by life at the moment and have a longing to escape, or alternatively you may feel that life is full of anxiety and insecurity and you crave safety.

Independence is frightening sometimes, as it implies separation and loneliness. Indeed, independence can be a lonely path, for we fear that by striking out on our own we may leave others behind. While this may be true, it is also necessary for our own growth to stand alone in this way. However, we also need to acknowledge that we need safety and stability in our lives. Without a certain basic level of security, our ability to function effectively is undermined. We float from one thing to another, and often from one person to another, without committing to anything. We need solid ground to build upon. Finding the balance between a secure environment and our need for independence and adventure is the challenge of the Asteroid Card. This is not an either/or choice. The Asteroid Card calls for a balance between our basic security needs and the higher aspirations of the soul. Fundamentally, this card symbolizes a kind of growing up, a coming to maturity. It offers us the chance to bring our lives into balance in a sophisticated way, but to do this we must often face our deepest fears. Some people are afraid of freedom and risk, others are afraid of commitment and dependence. Whichever side of the polarity frightens you most is the one you need to work on!

ACTIVITY: HEAVEN AND EARTH — A VISUALIZATION OF FREEDOM AND BELONGING

Stand in a quiet, darkened room with your eyes closed. Have your feet bare. Make sure you have plenty of space and you are not impeded by furniture or clutter. As you stand with your eyes closed, feel your feet on the ground. Spread your toes and allow your feet to really grip the floor. Feel the solidity of the ground beneath you. Imagine you are standing in a sunny green field. Feel how safe and grounded you are, see how wonderful and peaceful the weather is. Really imagine your environment in detail, and how you feel safe and supported by it. Now picture many strings radiating out from your body reaching down into the ground. Imagine that these strings are the only things that are keeping you on the ground, rather like the ropes mooring a hot air balloon. Now, imagine that one by one these strings are being released and gradually you float upwards and are free. If you feel uncomfortable or dizzy, just wriggle your feet and plant them even more firmly into the floor. Rise up slowly into the air and start to fly. Feel the exhilaration of flight and notice the perspective it gives you. Feel the light of the sun on you and try to see as far and as clearly as you possibly can. What does this expansion of perspective do for you? Does it make you anxious or afraid? Or does it inspire and excite you? Slowly return to the same place where you took off. Imagine yourself sinking gently back down to the ground. Make sure you have 'landed' properly by wriggling your feet again and planting them firmly into the ground. Recall your safe, sunny environment and fully realize that you have returned to it safely. When you are ready, slowly open your eyes. Write down your experiences, particularly noticing how easy or difficult it was for you to take off and land.

SATELLITE
Keyword: Attraction

BACKGROUND: Satellites are moons that orbit around the planets of the Solar System. They vary greatly in size, from a few kilometres in diameter to the size of a small planet. So-called true satellites are thought to have formed at the same time as the planets they orbit, whereas smaller satellites are probably asteroids that have been captured by the planet's gravity. The Earth's satellite, the Moon, remains something of a mystery. It is now thought to have formed very early in the history of our Solar System, from the debris produced when a wayward planet hit the Earth.

INTERPRETATION: A satellite is perpetually kept in orbit around its planet by the strength of the planet's gravity. Gravity attracts the satellite and keeps it there. It is this power of attraction that is described by the Satellite Card. This is not only sexual attraction, but all forms of that mysterious power that brings people together. It is hard to say what attracts us to other people. We can say that certain traits and aspects of physical appearance make someone desirable to us, but the process is really far more complex than that. Some people just seem to pull us into their orbit through sheer charisma and strength of personality, whereas others may attract us because of beliefs or ideals that coincide with our own.

If the Satellite Card appears in your reading then this power of attraction is being particularly activated at the moment. The source of the attraction may be a person, an idea, a project, or a group of people. If you draw the Satellite Card, start by identifying what it is about the situation that is attracting you, as it may not always be immediately clear. The process of attraction often takes place at an unconscious level and it can seem a complete mystery to us why a particular person attracts us. Once you have attempted to identify the source of the attraction, try to ascertain why this person or group or situation is attracting you right now. What qualities do they embody? Do you find these qualities admirable or reprehensible? We are often attracted by people who carry certain qualities that we do not acknowledge in ourselves — these people mirror the qualities back to us and can often have much to teach us. This can sometimes seem almost perverse. It is a common pattern in relationships to be attracted to the very same type of person who will cause one pain repeatedly, until the lesson is learned. People can become caught in cycles of abusive relationships where they unconsciously reproduce the same painful pattern. It is difficult to watch those we care for repeating these patterns obliviously — it is even more difficult when we experience this situation ourselves.

Consequently, it is very important to respect the power of attraction in our lives and bring it into consciousness. By honouring the mystery of attraction and examining it with honesty, we can begin to release ourselves from these painful patterns and learn the lesson that attraction is bringing to us. Try to be honest with yourself about this situation of attraction and honour the power of this force rather than resisting it.

ACTIVITY: HONOURING THE POWER OF ATTRACTION

Sit or lie down in a darkened room. Make sure that you have quiet and that you will be undisturbed. Close your eyes, relax and focus your attention inward. Form a picture of the person, group or situation that is attracting you. Imagine that they are giving off invisible waves of attraction. Now picture these waves gradually becoming visible. Notice the characteristics of the waves — colour, frequency, pattern and mood. Now allow the waves to slowly form themselves into pictures or things. Imagine the waves solidifying and condensing. What do you see? Don't worry if you don't see anything at all or if the pictures do not make sense; instead use your other senses. Are there any sounds or feelings associated with the waves? Can you reach out and touch them? Take your time to fully experience the qualities of these waves. You could also ask the person in your mind to tell you what qualities they embody for you. These qualities may seem to have nothing to do with the real person or group, but remember this is to do with what attracts *you*, the nature of your reality, not theirs. When you feel you have gathered all the information you can, slowly allow the waves to become invisible again and allow the person to gradually disappear. Return your attention to the room and open your eyes. Note down what you have experienced and look at the qualities embodied by the source of your attraction — can you find these qualities within yourself?

SOLAR SYSTEM
Keyword: Family

BACKGROUND: The Solar System is the name given to the system of nine planets, including the Earth, that orbit our sun. The planets vary greatly in size, composition and distance from the sun, but they all orbit in the same direction and in almost the same plane. This plane, or level of orbit, is known as the ecliptic. Pluto is the one exception to the rule — it has an orbit which is tilted by 18 degrees to the ecliptic. The planets of the Solar System probably all evolved at the same time. When the sun came into existence, a disk of gas and dust surrounded it. Some of this matter was blown away when the sun ignited and became a star, leaving the rocky planets Mercury, Venus, Earth and Mars to form. However, in the outer Solar System, some gas and dust remained and gradually condensed to form the gas giants Jupiter, Saturn, Uranus and Neptune.

INTERPRETATION: In the Solar System, all the planets are linked by one commonality — their orbit around the sun. So it is with families. All members of the family are linked, so that what affects a single member affects them all. The Solar System Card is rather like the Binary System Card in this way, but the Binary System Card deals with the link of a one-to-one relationship. The Solar System Card represents the many-to-many relationships that make up the family. Whatever kind of family we come from, their impact upon our lives is usually considerable. They say that blood is thicker than water and often we feel the pull of our family ties much more strongly than other ties in our lives. We do not choose our families and we may resent the ties that seem to bind us. There is a sense that we have no choice about our families, that they are somehow our fate and we just have to put up with them. Although we may love them dearly they can seem to restrict us.

If you draw the Solar System Card you are being reminded of the pull of your family ties. You need this group of people to support you, however you may feel restricted by them. The Solar System Card emphasizes the strength you can get from the support and love of your family, but it also stresses that, to some degree, you have no choice in the matter. You need to accept and love your family simply because they are there. Try to regard your family with respect rather than resentment — you may need them as much as they need you. Even if there is no sense of support or duty from either side, try to perceive the irrevocable link between you and the other members. This may be only the fact of your blood relationship to them. You may feel there is nothing else that links you, but this in itself is no small thing. Remember that the planets in the Solar System are vastly different, their only link being their orbit around the sun, but without the sun they never would have existed in the first place. Even if you dislike your family and are not close to them, try to see that they are or have been an irrevocable influence upon your life. The Solar System Card is asking you to accept the reality of that influence with grace.

ACTIVITY: PICTURING YOUR FAMILY

Draw a picture of your family as it was when you were five years old. Imagine you are a five-year-old as you draw. Use children's crayons or paints to help you get into the part. Let your imagination flow freely — artistic talent is not the point here. Remember to place yourself in the drawing or painting. It is better to work quickly, preventing your critical rational mind from imposing its judgement upon your work. When you have finished, go away and leave your picture. Do something totally unrelated and try not to think about what you have drawn. After an hour, come back and examine the picture. What does it tell you about your relationship with your family? Does the picture reveal anything about your feelings toward your family now, even though you are depicting it from a five-year-old's perspective? Pay particular attention to how you have placed yourself in relation to the other family members. Look at size, colours, distances between people and the chosen context of the picture. Write an analysis of the family represented by this picture. Do the contents of the picture surprise you, or is it pretty much what you expected? Try to refrain from being judgmental of yourself or other family members in your analysis. Are you happy with the results? Or does this picture alarm or upset you? Be particularly aware of the emotions that arise during this process. It is likely that these feelings originate in your early childhood — after all, you have taken a five-year-old's perspective.

COMET
Keyword: Transition

BACKGROUND: Comets originate in the outer reaches of the Solar System. They consist of a mixture of ice and dust formed into a snowball-like clump. This material is probably the leftovers from planet formation in the Solar System. A comet only becomes visible when the heat of the sun begins to melt the ice and the comet emits a stream of gas and dust. This forms the familiar head and tail of the comet — although most comets do not develop a tail. Sometimes a comet is captured by the sun's gravity and falls into a loose elliptical orbit. The most famous example of this kind of periodic comet is Halley's Comet which orbits the sun every 76 years.

INTERPRETATION: Life is not always as stable as we would like it to be. We may like the idea of change, but when it comes it is often unexpected and unwelcome. If the stability of our lives has been disrupted in some way, there usually follows a time of transition before things can settle down into a new pattern. The

Comet Card represents this time of transition. This is usually a temporary state, although the length of time we spend in transition can vary greatly. This often depends on the severity of the change we have experienced. Obviously, a major milestone in life such as a marriage or becoming a parent is likely to result in a longer period of transition. The life change we experience can also be drastic, such as the death of someone close to us. Painful experiences like bereavement can produce the longest and most profound periods of transition. It is always important to fully experience the time of transition, but particularly so if the change has been very painful. We may want to cling to any source of security and refuse to let go of what is changing in our lives, or simply deny that the change has affected us at all. All these strategies are a denial of the rite of transition symbolized by the Comet Card, and to deny this important stage in our lives is ultimately self-defeating.

Experiencing transition is an essential part of adapting to the changes in our lives and we may need to make extra allowances for ourselves during such times. If we try to carry on regardless, we will only end up prolonging the period of transition and making the whole experience more negative and uncomfortable. Transition need not be a bad time, although change often makes us feel anxious. It can be a very creative time, where new and exciting possibilities reveal themselves and we find ourselves doing things we would never have dreamed of before. Transition challenges our ability to adapt and prevents us from becoming too fixed and rigid in our ways.

ACTIVITY: A CEREMONY FOR CHANGE

Traditional societies often have set rituals to accompany major life transitions. These rituals also survive in our culture as wedding, funeral or coming-of-age rites, but they can often lack a real resonance for us. Whatever the transition you are experiencing, it may benefit you to perform a ritual to symbolize the change that is taking place. A ritual is a structured way of letting go of the old and allowing space for the new. It can take any form — a meal, a ceremony, a journey or visit — but it must be done with genuine intent and conviction. If you are moving house, for example, an appropriate ritual may be simply to clear out anything that you don't need that has been lying around in your old house and then to hold a house-warming dinner or party when you arrive at your new house. Many people do these things automatically, but it may be helpful to consciously design a ceremony for yourself or your family to formally acknowledge the transition you are making. This acts as a kind of 'signal' to the psyche that it is time to adapt to something new and it can make the time of transition an easier, more creative period.

STAR
Keyword: Stability

BACKGROUND: Although there is no such thing as a typical star, our own sun is a very ordinary, common-or-garden inhabitant of the universe. It is entirely unremarkable in that there are millions of other stars just like it, but it is essential to us on Earth as its light and heat ensures our survival. The sun is 4.5 billion years old; about halfway through its life. It will continue in much the same fashion for another 5 billion years and then, as its fuel becomes exhausted, will swell up to become a red giant. At this point the Earth will be engulfed by the sun's outer layers of material. Eventually, these outer layers will be blown off to leave a glowing remnant of the core. This tiny remnant — about the size of a large planet — will continue to shine as a white dwarf star.

INTERPRETATION: The creation and destruction of stars is a cataclysmic process, but the actual lifetime of stars like our sun is marked by a long period of stability. For the 10 billion years of its life, our Sun will shine steadily without any drastic changes or unexpected events. This stability has enabled the Solar System to develop and life on Earth to grow. We too need stability and regularity in our lives in order to develop and grow. Young children need a stable family environment to contain and nurture them. As adults, we need a baseline of structure and constancy to anchor our lives. After the uncertainty of transition as exemplified by the Comet Card, the Star Card represents a period of stability and tranquillity. If you draw this card, it represents a kind of reassurance with regard to the object of your enquiry. The Star Card indicates that the question you are asking is grounded in a firm grasp of reality and that you are fully aware of all the ramifications of the choice before you. It may also indicate that a stable environment is necessary for a resolution of your question and that you must embrace stability and ground yourself to find the answers.

ACTIVITY: CONTEMPLATING STABILITY IN THE NATURE OF A TREE

The best symbol of the kind of stability represented by the Star Card is a tree. Trees are firmly rooted in the earth, yet they are flexible enough to bend with the wind. It is their rootedness that allows them to stretch upwards toward the sun. Contemplate the flexible stability of the tree. Go for a walk and observe a real tree. Spend some time just looking at it and let yourself slowly absorb its nature. See what words come to mind as you become more aware of it. Take your time, for stability cannot be rushed. Try drawing or painting your tree, or writing down the words which exemplify its qualities for you. Finally, consciously try to absorb these qualities into yourself and see where they are already operating in your life, and where they are lacking.

BINARY SYSTEM
Keyword: Relationship

BACKGROUND: A binary system is a pair of stars linked by mutual gravity. They often rotate about each other and sometimes one star may strip material from another. Binary systems are thought to be very common in the universe, with possibly more than 50 per cent of all stars being part of multiple systems. Although multiple systems involving a number of stars are not unusual, binary systems of two companions are the most common. If one of the stars in the system reaches the end of its life and starts to throw off excess mass, the companion star may start to cannibalize the jettisoned material and increase its size. Therefore, a binary system involving a large star and a much more insignificant star may end up reversing itself. The large star dies and eventually becomes a tiny white dwarf, whereas the initially smaller star becomes beefed up with new fuel. Thus one companion's loss is the other's gain.

INTERPRETATION: Stars in binary systems are bound together. What affects one affects them both. This is the essential meaning of the Binary System Card — two people drawn together in a relationship which affects and changes them both. The relationship becomes greater than the sum of its parts and the two people in it are linked together in a unique and magical way. This occurs in any kind of relationship from a business partnership to a friendship, but the most intense kinds of relationships are with those we love — partners, parents, children. The nature of the bond in these relationships is much stronger and more binding. It is often the case that the strength of the bond is also in direct proportion to the perceived problems caused by the relationship. A bond can seem restrictive and we often push against our feelings of dependency or need for another.

Although dependency is often seen as negative, and indeed over-dependency on another person is debilitating, all relationships have some degree of mutual dependency implicit in them. This is exemplified by the Binary System Card. If you draw this card, you are being reminded of your need for another. We don't like to think of ourselves as dependent, we idealize the independent and free, but the Binary System Card reminds us that it is not always possible to live an ideal. We all need love and support, and we all benefit from giving love and support. This card asks us to remember the support we get from our relationships and that we may need another to help us in the area of our inquiry. It may indicate that we must swallow our pride and ask for help from someone we trust, for we cannot answer this question alone.

ACTIVITY: ASSESSING YOUR RELATIONSHIPS

Make a list of all the people with whom you have close relationships. For each person on the list, write down all the positive attributes of the relationship in one column and all the negative attributes in a second column. When you have done this for the whole list, look back over what you have written. Are there any recurring themes? This could indicate that the pattern of behaviour is more to do with you than the other person. Are there more negatives than positives for any people on the list? If so, what sustains your relationship with them? Looking at the positive things you get from your relationships, how could you thank your loved ones for what they give you? How could you approach transforming the negative patterns in your relationships? How could this be done in a way that honours and respects both sides? These are not easy questions, and often there is no simple answer, but this process of auditing our relationships can be very revealing. It is a valuable exercise which exposes the often unconscious patterns of our behaviour in relationship. This process can help us become more conscious of our relationship patterns, both positive and negative. Finally, for each person on the list write down one thing you could do to improve your relationship with that person. Set yourself a deadline for achieving your chosen aim. Be realistic — do not set yourself over-ambitious goals. In six months, look at the list again and note which aims you achieved, along with any changes in the relevant relationships.

STAR CLUSTER
Keyword: Friends

BACKGROUND: Stars often occur grouped together in densely packed clusters. Some of these star clusters are extremely large and ball-shaped. These are known as globular clusters and are among the oldest phenomena in the universe. They contain only old stars and probably many red giants (dying stars). There are also smaller, younger star clusters. These are known as open clusters because they are less dense and ball-like, forming a loose asymmetrical grouping. The best-known of these is the Pleiades, which is visible to the naked eye, although only six of the many hundreds of its stars can be discerned without a telescope. Because of their dense grouping, star clusters are prime sites for discovering exotic phenomena such as pulsars. The stars' proximity to each other means that any stellar event has a dramatic effect on the neighbours.

INTERPRETATION: Like the Solar System Card, the Star Cluster Card describes the complex interactions and hierarchies of a group, but whereas we cannot choose our families, we can certainly decide who we choose to call our friends. Often the link of friendship comes from early in our lives. We may have known many of our friends since school days. We also tend to develop friendships in areas of mutual interest or passion. If we are very interested in art, for example, we are more likely to form friendships with those who share our interest. Usually, our group of friends is a mixture of ties and loyalties from our early lives, our working lives and our personal interests. Some of us may have a wide-ranging and eclectic group of friends, whilst others may have just a few very close friends. Whatever the make-up of the group, our friends hold a unique place in our lives.

Without the intensity of a relationship or the sense of obligation and collective history connected with our families, our friendships are often the place in life where we are most free to be ourselves. If you draw the Star Cluster Card, you are being encouraged to examine the nature and value of your friendships. This may pertain to a particular friendship, or it may affect your attitude to all your friends. Do you truly trust and value them? Can you turn to them in times of need, or are they mostly of the 'fair weather' variety? The Star Cluster Card indicates that it is time to re-evaluate your friendships and your own attitude to your friends. If you have taken your friends for granted, now may be the time to more openly express your appreciation for their support. If you feel your friends are only there for the good times, then it may be time to examine your own behaviour as well as theirs, for our friends are a mirror for our own attitudes, beliefs and values. How we choose our friends can tell us a lot about ourselves. If we surround ourselves with superficial people, or people who do not truly value who we are, then that may indicate that we too do not want to look deeply at things, or that we have a low sense of self-worth.

Because of the element of choice in forming a friendship, our friends can be a far truer mirror of where we are in life than our families. In evaluating our friendships, we are in a sense evaluating and reflecting upon our own identity.

ACTIVITY: UNDERSTANDING YOUR OWN FRIENDSHIP 'CLUSTER'

Examine the picture of a Star Cluster on this card. Now imagine that you and your friends are a similar kind of cluster and draw a picture of yourself and your friends as this symbolic cluster. Putting yourself at the centre, draw in each of your friends, putting your closest friends closest to you and then working your way out. You can use stick figures or symbolic drawings. Better still, let your feelings for each particular friend guide your hand to draw an abstract shape to represent them. Use different coloured crayons and try to choose a colour that feels right for each person. Do not concern yourself too much with aesthetics — you are trying to contact your feelings and emotions about your friends, not to produce a work of art! When you have finished, examine how your friendships cluster around you. Is it a tight-knit group of very similar people, or a loose, diverse association? Are there any emphases or imbalances? What areas in the cluster do you feel most and least happy with? What can you do to redress the balance?

RED DWARF
Keyword: Self-doubt

BACKGROUND: A red dwarf is a star of low mass. Its characteristic red colour is an indicator of its cool surface temperature. If you take a burning ember from a fire, it glows yellow and then red, turning a deeper red as it cools. Red dwarf stars work on the same principle. Stars in the middle temperature range appear yellow, like our sun, whereas very hot stars appear blue. Red dwarf stars also tend to be small, hence the name. Size can range from half the size of our sun to smaller than the planet Jupiter.

INTERPRETATION: A red dwarf star may appear very small and insignificant next to its more flashy companions in the universe, and the Red Dwarf Card symbolizes this sense of inadequacy. It represents a feeling of insignificance or lack when we compare ourselves to others. We doubt our own abilities and we lack the confidence to act positively. Life may conspire to make us feel small in a situation, or we may habitually put ourselves in this position, suffering from a chronic feeling of lack of self-worth.

If the Red Dwarf Card appears it is telling you that an element of self-doubt has crept into the area of your inquiry. Even the most confident among us may come to doubt themselves from time to time — indeed a little self-doubt is probably healthy — but more often it is crippling and restrictive to our lives. The Red Dwarf Card indicates that it is time to reconcile your self-doubt and to move beyond it. Remember, a red dwarf star is no less a star because it is smaller than others. Size is not everything! It is not easy to conquer self-doubt, but try to keep it in proportion. Everyone else is not perfect and wonderful compared with you, they too may feel insignificant and small but hide it under a veneer of confidence. Don't make comparisons with others but focus on your own uniqueness and your own will. Try to be philosophical about your feelings of self-doubt and remember that everybody has them. They are an essential part of being human.

ACTIVITY: A RITUAL TO RELEASE SELF-DOUBT
Choose a small stone or pebble — preferably one you have found yourself — to represent your feelings of insignificance and self-doubt. Sit with your pebble and 'charge' it with all your doubting emotions by recalling incidents where you have allowed yourself to feel small or where you have doubted yourself. Let your

pebble represent the cluster of emotions which you know as your own self-doubt. Really spend time pouring all those negative feelings into that pebble. Now wash the pebble in clean, cold water. Holding it under a cold tap is ideal. As you perform this ritual washing, imagine that all your feelings of self-doubt are being cleansed away. Keep washing until you feel that everything has gone, has been released. Now bury the pebble in the earth overnight. If you do not have a garden, the earth of a house plant will do. Take the pebble out the following morning and wash it again. Keep the pebble as a reminder that, once you have released these feelings, an essential, indestructible part of you remains. Repeat this ritual with the same pebble whenever you feel it necessary. Remember, the greater intent and conviction you can put into this ritual, the more powerful the sense of release you will experience.

BROWN DWARF
Keyword: Failure

BACKGROUND: Brown dwarfs are under-achieving stars that fail to sustain nuclear fusion, the mechanism that enables a star to shine. They form in the same way stars do, condensing out of a cloud of hydrogen. However, they do not accumulate enough mass and cannot generate sufficient heat to maintain the necessary fusion process. They are often small, some not much larger than the planet Jupiter, and are obviously rather faint objects. Indeed, it is only with the help of powerful telescopes that astronomers have actually been able to find brown dwarfs, although their existence has long been theorized.

INTERPRETATION: People tend to be afraid of failure. In our society, to fail is seen as unacceptable. The very word has become pejorative and denotes someone who is a loser, a sad case whom others do not want to associate with for fear that the failure will somehow rub off on them. Success is rewarded and brings recognition, acceptance and love. Failure puts one beyond the pale. Yet to fail is an essential part of being alive. Without failure there would be no success, no sense of achievement, no lesson learned. It is a truism that we can learn more from our failures than from our successes. This is easy to say, but much more difficult to live. Our attitude to our own failures, and to those of others, is one of the true tests of life.

If the Brown Dwarf Card appears, it is indicating to you that you may be tested in some way by an experience of failure. This may be your failure or another's, or it may be the failure of a group project or idea. Whatever the area of your enquiry, the Brown Dwarf Card is warning you that the experience of failure will be an integral part of the answer. This does not mean that you should give up on the area of your enquiry, but it does indicate that things may not turn out as you expect, and that you may experience frustration and disappointment.

However, the Brown Dwarf Card is also a gift. It is offering you an opportunity to grow and mature, but it is not offering you an easy answer or quick solution. It is up to you and you alone to take the test of failure. No-one else can do it for you.

ACTIVITY: CELEBRATING YOUR FAILURES
An important part of dealing with our failures is accepting responsibility for them. Think of any areas of your life where you have experienced failure and make

a list of these failures. Look at the list and for each failure write down all the things you feel you learned from the experience. Imagine how your life would be if you hadn't learned any of these things. Create a fair copy of the list, making it look as smart as you can. Make it into a kind of certificate, like a qualification. You could even frame it! Keep your 'certificate' in a prominent place to remind you of what you have gained from failure. Remember you may need to update it from time to time.

RED GIANT
Keyword: Inflation

BACKGROUND: A red giant is a star which is in the process of dying. Stars sustain themselves through nuclear fusion reactions, fuelled by hydrogen. When a star has used up its supply of hydrogen, its fusion process gradually ceases and the star swells up to many times its original size. Loss of fusion also means a dip in the dying star's surface temperature, hence its red appearance. Eventually the star's core will collapse and the red giant will become a tiny white dwarf star not much bigger than a planet. This will be the fate of our own sun in about 5 billion years time.

INTERPRETATION: Red giants may look big and impressive, but their size is misleading. They are actually in the process of dying and their swollen size indicates they have run out of fuel. If you draw the Red Giant Card, something about the object of your enquiry is fooling you. There may be an aspect of the situation, or a person involved, that may seem hugely important and powerful, but really they are not. The importance of this person or situation has become inflated in your mind out of all proportion. This inflation may take the form of a seemingly insurmountable obstacle. There seems no way out, and you become possessed by the idea of this obstacle and the frustration it causes you. Again, you are being fooled. The Red Giant Card indicates that the obstacle is not as much of a problem as you believe. It has only become insurmountable in your own mind. You have inflated it into a size which seems utterly defeating.

If the Red Giant Card applies to a person, this person has an inflated sense of their own importance. You have been taken in by their egotism and you may need to look beyond the outer show. What really lies behind it is probably much more insignificant. The Red Giant Card may also be indicating that it is you who have become inflated and self-important with regard to your enquiry. You may secretly feel lacking in confidence or energy, but you have over-compensated by being excessively bombastic or egotistic. Examine your feelings honestly, and try to look at the situation with a sense of its true proportion.

ACTIVITY: WE'RE OFF TO SEE THE WIZARD!
Remember the story of the Wizard of Oz? The Wizard was supposed to be an all-powerful being who could do anything. He was the only one who could get Dorothy back to Kansas. He had a terrifying, booming

voice and frightened all his subjects. But really he was an insignificant, frightened little man hiding behind some smoke-and-mirrors tricks which made him seem imposing. And he didn't have any power. Remember the Wizard when you come across the person or situation represented by the Red Giant Card. Visualize that person and imagine that inside there is really an insignificant and frightened person at the controls. When you examine that situation, imagine that it is all a trick to mislead you and make you think it is important. Visualize the sleight of hand involved and then take the trick apart to see how it works. Determine that you will not be fooled again. Remain sceptical in the face of such inflation. Always keep the small, frightened little man behind the image in mind.

WHITE DWARF
Keyword: Essence

BACKGROUND: A white dwarf is a kind of stellar corpse, the remnant left after a small-to-medium sized star has died. When a star reaches the end of its life it runs out of fuel and starts to expand. It grows to many times its original size and turns red as it cools, becoming known as a red giant. After this stage, the star throws off all its layers of material and the core collapses to become a tiny but bright object the size of a large planet. Over the next few billions of years, the white dwarf will use up its remaining energy and gradually dim to become a dark lump of matter known as a black dwarf.

INTERPRETATION: After the inflationary stage described by the Red Giant Card, the collapsed star is reduced to its very essence, its core. Although the white dwarf is very small, it is also very bright and shines much more brightly than planetary objects of a similar size. The White Dwarf Card signifies a kind of stripping down to the bare essentials, the kernel of meaning beneath the layers of accumulated stuff.

When the White Dwarf Card appears you must look to the very heart of the matter and determine its essence. Whatever your question or object of enquiry, look at it in its barest and most fundamental terms. You are being asked to examine the real truth of the matter beneath the hyperbole, euphemism and good manners. The White Dwarf Card may indicate that you are missing the point in some way and that you need to look more clearly at what is really going on. To achieve an understanding of the essence of a situation, you can call upon the clarity and focus exemplified by the White Dwarf Card. Look at the situation and try to discern the one dominant theme or concern behind the complexity or confusion. The White Dwarf Card may also indicate that you have become too elaborate or made things too complicated with regard to your enquiry. You must strip things back to bare essentials by working out what is really important here and discarding the rest. You may be required to have a mental or physical clearing out process, throwing out what you don't really need and paring things down to a sleek, adaptable minimum.

ACTIVITY: SPACE CLEARING

A good way of learning to strip things down to their essence is to do it in a literal way. Have a clear-out and discard all those old clothes and bits and pieces that you have been holding on to. As you choose items to throw out, look at each one and ask yourself if this object expresses your essence as it is now. Although an object may have nostalgic associations that make you want to hold on to it, its time may have passed. Keep only what is useful to you here and now. Give the rest to charity, as someone else may need your discarded items. What emotions does the throwing out process bring up for you? How easy was it to make the decisions? Did you feel differently about yourself afterwards? Which items did you feel most expressed your essence? Make a note of these. Now think about all the people you know. What physical items represent their essences to you? Why? By making physical the process of identifying essence, you will be enhancing your ability to perceive the essence of things on all levels.

BLACK DWARF
Keyword: Change

BACKGROUND: When a star of moderate size comes to the end of its life, it expands to become a red giant. Eventually the star collapses to become a very small but very luminous white dwarf. The white dwarf will slowly fade over time to become a dark, inert blob known as a black dwarf. Because this fading process takes many billions of years, it is thought that the universe is too young to contain black dwarfs and so they remain theoretical objects. However, in the far future many billions of stars will meet this fate and the universe will be full of black dwarfs.

INTERPRETATION: There are many different types of change we encounter in the course of life, but all change is a kind of death. As well as the literal death of the body there are the symbolic deaths that we all experience as an integral part of life. The Black Dwarf Card is concerned with this concept of change as a symbolic death process. This does not connote literal death and should not be regarded with undue apprehension. Yet even the symbolic deaths we experience fill us with unease and fear.

The appearance of the Black Dwarf Card indicates that we may have to accept the death of some part of the object of our enquiry, whether that be the death of a relationship, an ideal or a treasured goal. Part of this process is letting go, and that often makes us feel afraid and insecure. Although we may know that a change must be made, we may still cling to the part of ourselves which is dying through holding on to the object or person concerned. Letting go can feel like a kind of death. We feel lost, confused, on the edge of a great abyss or void. Yet we must honour our fear and experience the void, for only by clearing away what is dead can we make room for something new to be born. Once we have faced the void, the 'long dark night of the soul', we emerge stronger and freer, ready to welcome the coming change.

ACTIVITY: A FIRE CEREMONY

On a piece of paper write the name of the idea, person or quality that you wish to let go of. On the same piece of paper draw a picture to symbolize what you have written. As you are preparing the piece of paper, feel deeply and fully the nature of the idea, person or quality concerned. Fold the piece of paper so that it is very small. Have a non-flammable container handy, with a lid. An old pan is ideal. Light a candle and then burn the piece of paper in the candle flame, with the intent that the act of burning will release the object concerned. Watch the paper as it burns and imagine that the flames are consuming your attachment. Feel that you are being released. Drop the burning piece of paper into the pan. When the paper has burnt, cover the pan with the lid. Take the ashes into your garden and bury them in the earth. If you do not have a garden, rinse the ashes out of the pan under cold running water until all trace of them has drained away.

NOVA

Keyword: Growth

BACKGROUND: A nova is an eruption that takes place on a star which is nearing the end of its life. This kind of eruption may be a one-off or it may occur repeatedly. For a nova to happen, the star must have some kind of intrinsic instability and it must also have a companion star in orbit around it. This means that novae only occur in binary or multiple star systems. The companion star's gravity pulls away matter from the star, sometimes in a dramatic manner. Novae can occur very suddenly, appearing and disappearing in a matter of days — an infinitessimally short period when we are dealing with the time frame of the universe.

INTERPRETATION: When a star becomes a nova, it can dramatically increase in brightness, flaring up for a few days and then gradually fading back to its original size and appearance. There are times in our lives when we too are required to shine brighter and exist with more intensity — these are often times when sudden challenges or crises come upon us. We are required to grow and meet the challenge that life has given us. As with a nova, our psychological growth tends to occur in sudden, dramatic spurts. There can be long periods of slow, unconscious development, as symbolized by the Planet Formation Card, but there are periods of life where sudden and exponential growth is needed. It is these times of challenge that are symbolized by the Nova Card. In the evolution of life on Earth, it is now believed that the process of evolution is not a slow, steady development over eons of time but instead is characterized by long periods of stability interspersed with sudden spurts of evolution and change. So it is with our psychological development.

If you draw the Nova Card, you are being alerted to the fact that you are entering one of these periods of sudden growth. This card represents an opportunity as well as a challenge. There is unprecedented potential in the Nova Card if you are willing to meet it. This is not a time to sit on your laurels and go for the safe option. Indeed this may be a time of great anxiety for you. All that you believed about yourself and about life seems in a state of continual flux. You may feel like retreating into a safe corner and hiding, but to get the most out of this time, you must stand up and look life squarely in the face. You are being challenged to expand your sense of who you are, to develop your potential and to embrace the entirety of yourself. In order to do this, you must let go of any restricting beliefs you have about yourself. These beliefs may be safe and comfortable, but they are holding you back. It is this letting go of restrictions that produces anxiety in many of us. However, coping with anxiety and fear is part of the growth process represented by this card. If you can accept your fear without letting it rule you, whilst at the same time embracing this time of growth, then you can truly fulfil the potential represented by the Nova Card.

ACTIVITY: FINDING AN INNER WARRIOR

In times of accelerated growth we may feel anxious and afraid, but we need to stand up, assert ourselves and make the most of the opportunities offered to us. The qualities we need are those symbolized by the warrior. Although we probably will not need to literally fight for our survival, on a symbolic level battle may need to be joined, even if the battle is taking place within ourselves. This is a time to stand up and be counted, and for that we need a certain inner strength and self-belief. Think of warrior figures from history, mythology, or popular culture. Is there any particular one that you most admire? Take some time to think or research this. Think back to your childhood — who were your heroines and heroes? Examples of positive warrior figures may range from goddesses such as Artemis or Athena, or real people like Martin Luther King or Nelson Mandela, who fought for their beliefs and their freedom, to figures from popular culture such as Batman and Superman, or the Star Wars characters, who embody the heroic figure to many in our society. Think carefully about who embodies the warrior spirit for you. Once you have chosen a figure that resonates for you, think about their story, their characteristics, their behaviour in times of crisis. What is it that you admire about them? Are you prepared to acknowledge these admirable characteristics in yourself? If not, what would it take to become a little more like your heroine or hero? Obtain a picture or model of your chosen warrior, or better still, draw them. Keep the picture or model in a prominent place to remind you of your own warrior abilities. Call on your warrior figure to help you in times of difficulty. Imagine they are with you, helping you through with their quiet support when you feel overwhelmed by fear or anxiety.

SUPERNOVA
Keyword: Culmination

BACKGROUND: A supernova is a dramatic event which is part of the death throes of a large star. Stars about ten times the size of our sun will suffer this fate. A star reaches the end of its life when it uses up its supply of hydrogen fuel. The nuclear reaction in its core, which sustains the star, begins to change as the hydrogen runs out. The star swells up as its core simultaneously shrinks. This increases the heat and mass in the core and leads to other fusion reactions involving helium, carbon and eventually iron. At this point the star's core collapses and there is a dramatic explosion as the star's outer layers are flung into space. The core may survive as a neutron star or pulsar, or may even collapse to form a black hole.

INTERPRETATION: There are times when events in our lives reach a point of crisis. There is a dramatic moment of release, an outburst or a sudden, unexpected event. These dramatic moments can be both high and low points in our lives. They may be moments of the greatest inspiration or the deepest despair. Either way, they are infinitely surprising and often totally unexpected. An explosion of realization and enlightenment or, equally, rage and horror, sweeps all other considerations aside.

If you draw the Supernova Card you are being put on alert that such a crisis point is being reached with regard to your enquiry. The critical time symbolized by the Supernova Card is highly creative and energizing. Drawing this card indicates that a huge amount of energy is being poured into the situation. This can be positive, but supernova explosions are also very dangerous. If you draw the Supernova Card, you are being warned to prepare for the approaching crisis and to take measures to protect yourself. Although the Supernova Card indicates a sudden and unexpected event, such crises do not just appear out of nowhere. It is likely that the explosion has been building for a long time. If you have drawn the Supernova Card with other cards, look at the surrounding cards to describe the root of the situation. If the Supernova Card indicates a crisis that has already happened, look to the other cards for the best way of reaping the ultimate benefit.

ACTIVITY: RELAXATION IN TIMES OF CRISIS

Although supernova events can ultimately be creative, they can be destabilizing in the short term. If you draw the Supernova Card, it is important to begin preparing for the coming crisis and to protect yourself from the fallout. The best way to do this is to remain as grounded as possible. One of the best ways of doing this is, quite literally, to lie on the ground. Find a quiet place, ideally outside in nature somewhere, but if this is not possible a quiet room in your house. Lie on your back on the floor or ground with your arms at your sides, palms down, and your legs stretched out. Gradually allow your body to relax and imagine you are sinking into the ground, becoming part of the ground. Imagine all your cares, worries and anxieties flowing out of you into the ground. Imagine you are 'earthing' all the turbulent energy within you, much like an electrical current automatically seeks to earth itself. At the same time, imagine you are absorbing the quiet strength and resilience of the earth. Repeat this exercise daily, or whenever you feel the crisis is becoming too much for you to handle. You may not avert the explosion, but you will be enhancing your ability to deal with it with equanimity.

NEUTRON STAR
Keyword: Intensity

BACKGROUND: A neutron star is a kind of remnant left over after a star has died. However, it takes a very large star — much larger than our sun — to create a neutron star. This kind of star's initial fate is to explode dramatically as a supernova. After this explosion, the core collapses to form an extremely dense and extremely small object. The neutron star is the densest form of matter known to exist. It is so compressed that a piece of it small enough to hold in your hand would weigh as much as a whole fleet of ships. This extreme density means that normal matter is squeezed into subatomic particles. The star's core is made up of neutrons (hence its name), surrounded by other particles such as protons and electrons. The whole thing spins very fast, emitting charged particles which are spun around to give off radio waves.

INTERPRETATION: There are times when we become intensely focused upon a project or an idea to a degree where everything else is blotted out from our minds. There are also times when we feel intense passion for another person, or for a principle, and we cannot be gainsaid or diverted from our intended course. It is this kind of intensity that is represented by the Neutron Star Card. We may feel driven by our intensity of focus and also exhilarated by it. If we are working on a creative project, this intensity may be highly productive and rewarding. If we feel intense passion for a person this can also be deeply moving and fulfilling. However, the danger with such intensity is that it can spill over into obsession. The blotting out of all other concerns, if prolonged, can result in a narrowing of focus and a skewed perception of reality. Periods of intensity in our lives can be rich, productive times. But prolonged, unproductive and frustrating periods of intensity can throw us off balance.

If you draw the Neutron Star Card, the object of your enquiry is filled with this intense energy. It may be the intensity of your own feelings, or the feelings of another, or it may be that your enquiry arouses intense emotions by its very nature. It is important that you find some productive release for the intensity and use your unusual clarity and focus for a positive end. If you have intense feelings for another person and circumstances dictate that they cannot be expressed, try not to become bitter or obsessive. It is important that you find an outlet for your emotions in a way that does not hurt others. Remember, many creative people have found that the frustration of an intense passion for another has been the fuel which has fired them to do their best work. This is not an easy situation, but it is important to both contain and honour your intense feelings without either repressing them or acting them out in ways that cause injury to others.

ACTIVITY: FINDING BALANCE IN TIMES OF INTENSITY

To get the best out of a period of intensity in your life, it is important to remain balanced. Whatever the nature of your intense focus or emotion, try to find an activity that is the direct opposite or complement of it. For instance, if you are intensely involved in a project that involves a lot of sitting and writing, make time for walking and exercising in the open air. This may be the last thing you feel like doing, but it is often the last thing you want to do that is the very thing you need. If you have an intense passion for a person, try to spend time with lots of other people and start to examine people around you. See things from their point of view. In these situations, we often get locked into our own perception of the desired other. It is therefore important to experience others' worldviews at this time, as we may feel that ours is the only one that exists or matters. Whatever activity you try, if you feel that it is extremely boring and you really are not in the least interested in it, then you have probably found the right one! Persist, and you will find a valuable counterbalance to the fires of your intensity.

PULSAR
Keyword: Structure

BACKGROUND: Pulsars are a variety of neutron star that pulse at a regular rate. All neutron stars rotate, but if the star has a strong magnetic field which has a different axis to its axis of rotation then the radio waves it emits appear to sweep across the sky in a regular pulse, rather like a lighthouse. Astronomers now think that pulsars are young neutron stars and that non-pulsing neutron stars are either old pulsars or their weaker magnetic field may mean that they never became pulsars. Pulsars pulse at an extremely regular rate and sometimes very fast — around 1,000 times a second.

INTERPRETATION: The regularity at which pulsars rotate makes them inherently predictable. We know that they will continue to behave in this fashion for the foreseeable future. We can time each pulse and know that each future pulse will be at the same rate. This characteristic of predictability and regularity is an important part of the way we structure our lives. We all need a certain amount of structure in our everyday lives and we all develop habits of behaviour which impose this kind of structure. We may have habits and rituals which we perform each morning, a getting-up routine which may be as simple as making a cup of coffee. These habitual behaviours make us feel secure and provide an anchor in our lives. There are also structures that are imposed on us in life — for example, having to work from 9 to 5, Monday to Friday — which we may perceive as both comforting and limiting.

The Pulsar Card symbolizes the structure and routine of our lives. Drawing this card indicates a need to formulate a structured approach to the object of your enquiry. You may need to work out some form of system for dealing with the situation. Structure imposes limits upon us and without limits we can never build anything in this world. However, we may sometimes battle against the limits that we feel have been imposed on us from outside. The Pulsar Card may indicate that we feel limited or trapped by the structures imposed on us, but that they are nevertheless crucial to the object of our enquiry. We need to co-operate with the energy exemplified by the Pulsar Card and find a system or structure that is flexible and that works for us, without making us feel imprisoned.

ACTIVITY: IDENTIFYING YOUR HABITS

Think of your own habitual behaviours and write down as many as you can. These could be very small things, like the way you prefer to drink your tea or coffee. They may be things that you do only occasionally or many times a day. For each habit, note how long you have been following this behaviour. Record why you think you have developed this habit and how it makes you feel. Is there a common thread that links any of your habits? Are any of them addictive or damaging to your health, like smoking? How do you feel if you are prevented from any of your habitual behaviours? Habits are not bad, indeed they are necessary, but we sometimes become too dependent on them and too inflexible. Try to identify what you feel are your most positive habits and how they make you feel. Is there a way you can substitute any of your bad habits with your good ones?

NEBULA: STAR BIRTH
Keyword: Creation

BACKGROUND: Nebula is a Latin word for cloud and that is exactly what nebulae are — vast clouds of dust and gas which act as nurseries for new stars. Clumps of this stellar dust, often the remnants of supernova explosions, gradually condense into a dark mass. The clumps' increasing mass creates increasing gravity, which in turn causes the whole thing to collapse. This process is pushed along by the shock waves which are the aftermath of supernova explosions. Thus the death of one star helps to ignite the birth process of another. At this stage, the clump becomes a protostar, the condensing process causing the temperature to rise dramatically. When the protostar is hot enough, nuclear reactions begin and the new star begins to shine. However, only when the protostar can sustain nuclear fusion and achieve stability is it truly a new star. The ignited stars light up the surrounding dust and gas, creating the characteristic and often beautiful cloud formations of nebulae.

NEBULA: STAR BIRTH

INTERPRETATION: Nebulae depict the process of star creation and they are among the most stunningly beautiful phenomena in the universe. The process of creation in nebulae is slow and gradual, and in its early stages these clouds of gas are dark and unremarkable to the observer. However, the light of the forming stars begins to illuminate the surrounding gas clouds, creating beautiful patterns and formations.

The creative process often affects us in this way, filling us with awe at its beauty and magical power. If you draw the Star Birth Card, creativity is entering your life. The act of creation may manifest in any number of ways from the literal to the esoteric. Having a baby, for example, is an act of creativity in a physical sense. All creative projects follow the pattern of conception, gestation and production that mirrors this most basic and most important of human creations. The Star Birth Card may indicate that you are entering any one of these phases and is asking you to honour the entire process. Remember that the nebula, although beautiful, begins life as a dark cloud of congealing dust. Similarly, many creative endeavours begin in the dark, with little evidence of the beauty to come. Creative production requires sustained effort. After the wonders of the moment of inspiration (which is also indicated by the Supernova Card) there is the long slog of making our grand ideas a reality. Inspiration may fail and confidence falter. The Star Birth Card indicates that we may be in for a long haul, but ultimately this is a very positive card. The process of creation is one of the most meaningful experiences in life and one of the most rewarding.

ACTIVITY: FINDING A SYMBOL OF CREATIVITY
Lie down in a darkened room. Try to shut out any extraneous noise — it is important that the environment is as quiet as possible. Cover your eyes with a scarf or bandanna. Imagine you are floating in space among the beautiful clouds of a nebula. Observe the patterns and colours of the nebula, taking some time to enjoy its beauty. Now ask the nebula to give you a symbol of your creativity. Imagine that the symbol is slowly congealing out of the gas clouds, in exactly the same way as a developing star. When the symbol is fully formed, take it in your hands and examine it closely, noting colour, texture and size. Take as much time as you need. Finally, thank the nebula and slowly return to Earth, bringing the symbol with you. Really feel that you are bringing something back from outer space into this reality. Make a drawing or painting of the symbol. It is important that you do this immediately, while you still have the energy of the symbol 'in your hands'. This picture is now a talisman that can tell you much about the nature of your creativity. For example, if your symbol is a flame or a fire, your creative nature is probably fiery and unpredictable. On

the other hand, if your symbol is a cup of water, your creativity is of a more receptive, reflective kind. Keep this symbol in mind whenever you are called upon to create anything, no matter how small. It will also help you to reconnect to your creative source at times when you feel inspiration lacking.

NEBULA: STAR DEATH
Keyword: Transformation

BACKGROUND: A planetary nebula is a dust cloud that forms after a star has died. When the star's core collapses or the star explodes as a supernova, its outer layers are blown off into clouds which often form beautiful and intricate patterns. This type of nebula is called a planetary nebula to differentiate it from the nebulae associated with star birth. The name is a bit of a misnomer as planetary nebulae have no connection with planets or planet formation. The nebula shown in this card is the Hourglass Nebula, so called because the dead star may have a companion star whose gravitational presence helped push the gas and dust out into an 'hourglass' formation.

INTERPRETATION: Transformation in the form of destruction is an integral part of the cycle of life and death. We tend to believe that destruction is somehow unnecessary and avoidable, but without destruction there can be no creation. Nature itself can be destructive. Storms, fires, floods and hurricanes can all wreak havoc upon the land and upon people. Yet it has often been observed that in the aftermath of these destructive events, life springs up anew at an accelerated pace, as if it had been energized by the very violence of its destruction. The Star Death Card embodies this difficult, transformative energy that is so feared and yet so necessary to us. If you draw this card, there is some area of your life that needs a serious overhaul. It may seem an act of vandalism to tear everything apart, but if you draw the Star Death Card you may find you have little choice in the matter.

Like the Black Dwarf Card, this card embodies necessary change, but whereas the Black Dwarf Card focuses on change through letting go, here the emphasis is on change through transformation. If you can approach the object of your enquiry in this spirit, cooperating with the energy of necessary transformation, then you will find the Star Death Card easier to understand. Try to approach the process of destruction and transformation as consciously and positively as you can. It is important to be as proactive as possible. If you try to avoid or procrastinate, you may find that destruction is unleashed from an external source over which you will have no control. For example, you are tired of your job and need to change your way of working, but avoid doing anything about it because you fear a loss of security. You may suddenly find that you are made redundant or given different responsibilities which you find even more untenable. You are left wishing you had departed on your own terms. It is also important to remain conscious of the transformation process, or you may find destructiveness is unleashed in other areas of your life and inflicts hurt on innocent parties — usually the people we love the most. This is the most difficult aspect of the transformation process and is the reason we fear and avoid it. Paradoxically, it is our very fear and avoidance which creates the climate for uncontrolled and wanton acts of destruction. Therefore, if you cannot bring yourself to co-operate with this process for your own sake, remember that by doing so you will be helping the people you love most.

ACTIVITY: A RITUAL FOR TRANSFORMATION

Think of an area of your life that needs destruction and transformation. Draw a picture of it, or draw something that symbolizes it. If you do not feel comfortable with drawing, write a description in words. Look at the piece of paper and think of how you would like to destroy it. This could be simply tearing it up, or it could be by burning, or immersion in water, or burial in the ground. Once you have decided upon a method that feels right, destroy the piece of paper in your chosen way. Imagine that the chosen area of your life is being transformed by your symbolic destruction. How does it make you feel? What are you left with? Ashes? Shreds of paper? A wet mess? What could you do with what is left — apart from simply throwing it away! Remember that how you dispose of the remains is part of the transformation process. What lessons can you learn from this symbolic destruction? Write an account of the ritual, emphasizing the different feelings you experienced at each stage.

PLANET FORMATION
Keyword: Process

BACKGROUND: When stars are formed, coalescing out of gas and dust clouds called nebulae, there is some leftover matter which is ejected by the forming star. This cloud of matter forms a disk of dust which orbits around the new star, trapped by its gravity. This dust cloud is called a protoplanetary disk. Over time, the disk gradually coalesces to form planets. Our own Solar System was probably formed in this way. It is not known how many planetary systems there are in the universe, but the Hubble telescope has observed the formation of protoplanetary disks around stars in a nebula. This is the first step toward discovering planets that are like our own.

INTERPRETATION: We are usually good at understanding the beginnings and endings of things. We may also become adept at dealing with challenging circumstances in our lives. However, we are not so good at understanding the kind of invisible, inner churning that goes on as all levels of our consciousness process

PLANET FORMATION

what has happened. The Planet Formation Card represents this concept of process, where nothing much seems to be happening, but in actual fact crucial events are silently taking place within us. Anyone involved in a creative activity will know there is a period when they cannot communicate or manifest their ideas but during which there is a kind of unconscious gestation going on. It is sometimes difficult for us to know when this is happening and often we are totally unaware of it. We may get a vague sense of something happening, but we are not sure and we may tend to dismiss or ignore it. The clearest indications of process come to us in dreams, which may be particularly vivid at these times.

If the Planet Formation Card appears, it indicates that it is particularly important for you to honour your inner process. We are not used to valuing something so invisible in our literal-minded culture, but the Planet Formation Card tells us that what is happening is important, if not crucial, to our own development. If we cannot honour our inner process, we will find it much more difficult when the time comes to manifest the results of that process in the world. Think of the miracle of the growth and gestation of a baby. Usually, there is no indication to the outside world that a new life is forming (although the mother is all too aware of it!) until about four or five months into pregnancy. Yet it is during early pregnancy that the most crucial stages of foetal development take place.

ACTIVITY: KEEPING A DREAM JOURNAL

If you have drawn the Planet Formation Card, you are being put on alert with regard to your inner process. One way of keeping in touch with this process is to keep a dream journal. Keep a notebook or diary and pen beside your bed and write down any dreams you have immediately upon waking. Try to do this as soon after the dream as possible, as dreams fade and are forgotten very quickly. Review your journal weekly or at regular intervals. Look at any common threads in your dreams and try to see how they relate to your everyday life. Consult a dream dictionary to help you out with symbolism and interpretation. Describe your dreams to friends and family and ask them if they can see any meanings that you may be missing. Can you see any ways in which your dreams depict the nature of your inner process?

GALAXY FORMATION
Keyword: Organization

BACKGROUND: The formation of galaxies is a mysterious process that is still very little understood. This process occurred very early in the history of the universe, so we can only see galaxy formation at work today by observing very distant galaxies. This is because the light from these distant corners of the universe has taken so long to travel to us — billions of years — that what we are actually seeing is the universe as it was billions of years ago, very early in its life. What we see are many large star clusters, all very close together. It is now believed that galaxies form out of these star clumps through a complex series of collisions and mergers, gradually increasing in size and density until they take on their characteristic spiral shape.

INTERPRETATION: Galaxy formation is a slow process that unfolds organically over very long periods of time. It is a natural process that cannot be hurried, and so it is with the Galaxy Formation Card. This card represents order in the form of organization, a natural structuring that allows us to function in an optimum way. This type of organization is different from that represented by the Pulsar Card. It is not a structure imposed from the outside; it evolves organically. When we think of organizing our lives, we often think that this means imposing new routines and new behaviours upon ourselves, that our old way of doing things is bad and must be forcibly reformed. This is not the kind of organization represented by the Galaxy Formation Card. If this card appears for you it does indicate that you need to think about the way you organize your life, but in a positive, evolutionary way. In other words, you don't necessarily need to change everything, but it may be time for you to look at ways you can evolve beyond your current situation.

The Galaxy Formation Card is pragmatic — it is asking you to look at the tangible things in your life — but it also works at a deeper level. By examining your patterns of behaviour and evolving a more positive set of behaviours you are providing a better, healthier environment for your own inner development.

ACTIVITY: USING ACTIVE REMEMBERING TO ORGANIZE 'ORGANICALLY'

Take some quiet time to sit or lie down comfortably, closing your eyes. Spend a few minutes just relaxing and letting go of the pressures of the day — you could listen to some soothing music if this helps. Once you are starting to feel relaxed, take yourself back to what you were doing exactly a week ago. Start at the beginning of the day and try to remember everything you can about what you did during this day *in the order that it happened*. Try not to skip backwards and forwards; imagine that you are reliving the day as fully as you possibly can. If you keep a diary or a schedule, you could use this as a prompt. Move through the whole week in this way until you reach the present. Remember as much as possible, from the minutiae of living to the significant events that might have happened. Include any dreams in your remembering. Give equal weight to each thing that you remember — try not to make judgements about how you have spent your time. When you have completed the process of remembering, look at the week as a whole. What do your memories consist of? What type of things stick in your mind the most? Where are the gaps in your memory? How much of your time was spent in guilt, regret or rushing around like a headless chicken? Looking at the overview of your week, what could you change to improve the quality of your life?

This process of remembering can offer us a perspective on our lives that we can often lose in the daily grind. It gives us space to have an overview and can enable us to be more consciously pro-active in directing the everyday course of our lives in a natural way. This is not about being more efficient — think of it as an exercise in maximizing enjoyment. Don't plan anything specific, but over the following week, decide to increase the joy you get in every moment of your life. Try to remember this decision as often as possible during the week and then at the end of the week repeat the remembering process. Did you notice any difference? Carry on with the remembering process every week for as long as you like, keeping notes each time about what you did. Observe and record your behaviour and after a few weeks look back at your notes to see if a pattern emerges or if there have been any changes.

SPIRAL GALAXY
Keyword: Productivity

BACKGROUND: When we think of a galaxy, we will probably imagine a spiral galaxy. This type of galaxy has a ball-like nucleus surrounded by spiral arms which form a kind of halo around the centre. Our own galaxy, the Milky Way, is classed as a spiral galaxy and our sun is located towards the outer part of the galaxy, along one of the spiral arms. It is believed that spiral galaxies are the more youthful galaxies in the universe and that as they get older they increasingly condense into round blobs called elliptical galaxies.

INTERPRETATION: It is important for us to feel productive in our lives, whatever the nature of our work. Even if we do not have a job in the traditional sense, we need to feel that we are achieving something worthwhile with our time. If we do not believe in what we are doing at some level, we eventually become cynical and jaded. Unfortunately this is the case for many of us who feel we are in humdrum jobs where what we do seems meaningless and unsatisfactory. This can be the case even if we are well paid for our work, although good pay may serve to keep us in an unsatisfactory job for longer. However, many people work in not particularly well-paid jobs simply because they strongly believe in what they are doing. People who work in education, medicine or the charity sector, for example. But even in these worthwhile areas, many people have become very disillusioned about what they perceive as the negative changes of the last few years. Job satisfaction has become much more elusive in recent times.

The Spiral Galaxy Card indicates that a need to be productive and to be involved in something satisfying is being strongly constellated at the moment. Whatever activity you regard as your 'job' is under scrutiny at the moment, and the appearance of the Spiral Galaxy Card is asking you to examine how satisfied you are with the current situation. Do you feel you are as productive as you could be, or are you becoming dissatisfied and frustrated? The Spiral Galaxy Card indicates that these issues are paramount, and you may be required to put aside such issues as security and financial gain and prioritize your own sense of productivity and inner satisfaction about what you do.

ACTIVITY: A PRODUCTIVITY AUDIT

Write down everything you feel you have achieved in the past year. Go through the year on a month-by-month basis, and list the 'products' of your labours. These may not necessarily be tangible things — something like 'improved relationship with a friend or colleague' may be just as important as reaching a more quantifiable goal. These achievements need not necessarily be earth-shattering either. 'Getting the car fixed' may feel like a big success to some of us! When you have completed the list, review what you have written. Do you feel proud of your achievements? Are you happy with what you have produced? If not, what needs to change to help you become more productive? What didn't you do that you wish you had? With these questions in mind, write a set of targets for the coming year. Include all the things you wished you had done but didn't. Think about where you would like to be a year from now and set yourself a reasonable set of tasks for getting there. Again, these do not have to be weighty goals — 'spring cleaning the house' or 'shopping early for Christmas' are viable and achievable targets. Once you have written down your targets, review them at monthly intervals. Record your progress and make any necessary adjustments (but don't just keep putting things off!).

ACTIVE GALAXY
Keyword: Turbulence

BACKGROUND: Active galaxies are so called because they emit large amounts of radiation in the form of light, radio waves, gamma rays, x-rays, etc. All galaxies emit radiation to some degree, but some galaxies are considerably stronger sources than others and are therefore termed 'active'. The reasons for these huge emissions are thought to be quasars or black holes at the centre of the galaxies. The most active galaxies have quasars at their centre. These are incredibly bright, little understood phenomena that emit huge amounts of radiation. Less active, but very powerful at radio wavelengths, are galaxies which have a spinning Black Hole at their core. It is believed that active galaxies with quasars may be infant galaxies created soon after the Big Bang. These galaxies are so distant that it has taken billions of years for their light to reach us. What we are actually seeing is how the galaxy looked billions of years ago, in the early days of the universe.

ACTIVE GALAXY

INTERPRETATION: Drawing the Active Galaxy Card indicates that some disruption is entering your life. You may be in for a turbulent, unsettling time as you adjust to changes imposed on you by your environment. Although the turbulence indicated by this card is external, what you experience may cause you to react inwardly in many ways. You are likely to feel some anxiety or even fear. Your future is in the balance and if you resist change you may simply increase the level of anxiety for yourself. You may want to bury your head in the sand and try to pretend that nothing is happening, but denial will simply make the changes more difficult to deal with in the long run. Even if you feel you are being treated unfairly, try to meet this period of turbulence head on and embrace it. If you ride this time of turbulence with flexibility, much like a surfer rides a wave, you may find that ultimately this is a very creative period for you. Try to accept that you will feel rather anxious during this time, and stand back from the situation. View things in the long term. This will help you decide what to do and also when to act, for things cannot stand still in times of turbulence.

The Active Galaxy Card indicates that you need to act decisively in this situation, rather than remaining passive and hoping to preserve the status quo. By acting appropriately, at the right time, you will be able to ride the turbulence more smoothly. If you resist and deny, you run the risk of being swept away.

ACTIVITY: LEARNING FROM TURBULENCE IN NATURE

Observe how turbulence occurs in the natural world. For example, watch how birds make use of the unpredictable winds, or how waves crash upon the shore in stormy seas, or how trees bend in a gale. Birds of prey make use of wind patterns such as thermals to enable them to ascend and then hover motionless. Animals learn the patterns of turbulence in their element and then use them to their advantage. Think about, observe and learn the pattern of the turbulence that is occurring in your working life. Make a diagram or symbolic drawing of this pattern, remembering to include yourself in it. How can you take advantage of the turbulence? Choose an animal and observe or find out how your animal deals with turbulence in its natural environment. Write a strategy for dealing with the turbulence in your life based on the behaviour of your animal. Set practical goals and then consider how you can set about reaching them. If you refuse to be swept along with the tide, then how can make your resistance work? If you cannot resist the storm that is raging, then how can you best survive it intact?

ELLIPTICAL GALAXY
Keyword: Stagnation

BACKGROUND: Elliptical galaxies are the oldest type of galaxy in the universe. They are often round or blob-like in shape, hence their name. These galaxies formed soon after the Big Bang and they contain only old stars and many red giants. It is possible that one day all galaxies will end up as elliptical galaxies, as all the gas and dust which allows new star formation is used up. Elliptical galaxies can vary greatly in size. Some are the biggest galaxies in the universe, having a diameter of hundreds of thousands of light years, whilst others contain under a million stars and are hardly visible.

INTERPRETATION: Unlike active or spiral galaxies, elliptical galaxies have reached a very stable state. Many of the stars in these galaxies are coming to the end of their lives or are in the process of dying. In terms of the creation of new phenomena, not much is going on. Everything is just gradually fading away and nothing new or interesting is expected to happen. This is the state of stagnation represented by the Elliptical Galaxy Card. Everything has become just a bit too predictable and there is no new input into the situation. When we are in a state of stagnation in our working or personal lives it may feel comfortable and safe, but we are also likely to feel dissatisfied. There is something missing. Things are just a little too safe and predictable and we crave more excitement or creativity. We may feel that we are trapped in a state of stagnation and that we have little choice in the matter. If we remain in the situation of stagnation, we will find ourselves becoming less and less productive. We will fall into a kind of energetic slumber where we feel lacking in energy and disinclined to move, despite our unhappiness with the current situation.

If you draw the Elliptical Galaxy Card, the object of your enquiry has reached a state of stagnation. Nothing more can be gained from the situation. You must either introduce a new element into the equation or decide to move on. The situation of stagnation can be changed by the infusion of 'new blood' in the form of the introduction of new people or new ways of doing things. However, this is not always possible and it may be that you have already tried everything you can do to liven things up. In this case, you must simply take a deep breath and walk away. Moving out of a situation of stagnation is often difficult as you may feel unmotivated and lacking in energy. You are being

ELLIPTICAL GALAXY

drained by the situation and it is vital that you take some action, even if you cannot raise any enthusiasm for it or do not feel it will help. Simply taking action, however small or unsatisfactory, will help to release you from the heavy pall of stagnation. You will find that each step you take away from the situation will be taken more lightly and with greater ease.

ACTIVITY: A RITUAL FOR RELEASING STAGNATION

Obtain some modelling clay and form a shape or a model to represent your stagnant situation. This does not have to be a work of art, just allow your hands to form the clay without too much conscious intervention from your mind. When you are satisfied with your shape, allow the clay to dry naturally, or alternatively bake it in the oven. When the clay is completely dried through, place the object in a large, robust container, such as a bucket or washing-up bowl. Get a hammer and smash your object into small pieces. As you do this, imagine you are releasing yourself from the situation of stagnation. Keep going until you have reduced the object to small fragments or, ideally, dust! Put the dust or rubble into a container and take it to a high place. A hill or a bridge is ideal. Open the container and release its contents over the edge of the bridge or hill. You are releasing the symbol of your stagnation to the air. As you do this, imagine and intend that you are letting the air of change blow into the situation of stagnation. Imagine that the air is lightening your burden and releasing you. Doing this on a windy day is ideal. Make sure you dispose of all of the dust or remains. You do not want to hang on to the stagnant energy.

QUASAR
Keyword: Success

BACKGROUND: The word quasar is an acronym for quasi-stellar radio source, so called because of the powerful radio emissions that come from them. Quasars are incredibly distant, enigmatic objects that dwell at the centre of galaxies. They are relatively small — only a little larger than our own Solar System — but shine very brightly. The huge amount of energy emitted by quasars has baffled astronomers and their extreme distance has made them difficult to study. However, it is now believed that quasars are somehow powered by black holes, which explains the enormous levels of energy involved. Another recent theory is that quasars are created by the violent collision of two galaxies. Matter from the collision is flung off and swallowed by a black hole in the centre of one of the galaxies. This process somehow ignites the quasar. As the quasars which have been observed are very distant, some billions of light years away, it is thought that they could be phenomena that existed only in the early universe. This is because the light from these distant galaxies has taken several billion years to reach us. What we are seeing is the galaxies as they were all those billions of years ago, very early in the life of the universe.

INTERPRETATION: Quasars are among the brightest objects in the universe. They shine with an incredible power and intensity. On a human scale, this ability to shine and to be visible is what allows us to be successful in our lives.

The Quasar Card indicates public recognition and success with regard to your inquiry. This is more than a personal feeling of satisfaction and completion, it indicates a public and visible achievement. The Quasar Card may signify formal recognition such as gaining a qualification or winning an award or prize. It takes courage to stand up and be visible, to 'go public' with your project, your beliefs or your creations, and the Quasar Card indicates that you are being rewarded for this courage. You have shone as brightly as you possibly could and others have seen and benefited from what you have done. Enjoy this time while it lasts, for the success indicated by the Quasar Card can be transitory. It is a time of celebration, a peak of attainment to be relished to the full, but remember that this too will pass. Make the most of your success, but keep your feet on the ground. Relish this time of achievement and remember that the confidence that it gives you will serve you well in the future.

ACTIVITY: CREATING AN ALTAR TO SUCCESS
What symbols do you keep of your own personal success? Do you have trophies or certificates for academic, sporting or other achievements? Or do you have more personal symbols of your successful ventures? How do you treat these objects? Are they framed, polished, displayed and treated with care, or are they shoved in the back of a drawer somewhere? Consider that how you treat these symbols of achievement, however minor you consider these achievements, is an indication of your attitude to your own success. Make an altar and gather on it all the symbols of your achievements. This could be a shelf or a table or part of a wall. Clean your objects and make them look good. If you have no symbol for a particularly important success, create one. This could take any form, for example a drawing or a symbolic article such as a cup or crystal. When you have gathered all your symbols and placed them on the altar, consider each one and remember the situation which led you to be given this item. Are there any common strands that link the different occasions of success? Do you feel proud or embarrassed? How might the common strands of your past successes serve you in achieving success in the future?

BLACK HOLE
Keyword: Subjugation

BACKGROUND: Black holes are created as a part of the death process of a star. However, only the most massive stars (more than 30 times the size of our sun) are large enough to create black holes. When this kind of star reaches the end of its life, its core collapses causing a dramatic supernova explosion. Because of the star's size, it has a huge gravitational force. This pulls matter inward at such a rate that the star's core keeps on collapsing in on itself until it seems to disappear. Actually it becomes so infinitely small that it becomes what is known as a singularity — an object that has no dimension, but that is infinitely heavy and dense. The mass and density of the singularity create a gravitational field so strong that even light cannot escape. Hence the name black hole. Because space and time are connected, the black hole's immense gravitational field also has a warping effect upon time. If you were to approach a black hole, you would appear to slow down. The closer you got, the slower you would appear to move, until you came to a complete standstill. Time itself would seem to stop. The point at which this happens is known as the event horizon. This effect has led to theories linking black holes and time travel. However, this would be impossible in practice because the incredible forces surrounding the black hole would tear apart anything that approached it. Recent theories suggest that most galaxies have a massive black hole at their centre and that they are a key element in galaxy formation and quasar development.

INTERPRETATION: If you were to get too close to a black hole, its massive gravity would overpower you and pull you in. You would be helpless to resist and completely in its power. The Black Hole Card suggests that you have encountered a person or a situation which is far more powerful than you. The only choice available to you is subjugation to this more powerful force. In work situations we often rail against the power of our employer who can seemingly hire or fire us at will, or we may feel victimized by the behemoths of the establishment or the government. These institutions are too powerful for us to take on alone and we have no choice but to accede to the fact of their power over us. This does not mean to say one should not fight against injustice on the part of these institutions, but that we must all realize that we cannot take them on single-handed.

The Black Hole Card reminds us that we must recognize situations where it is just plain useless to fight against the inevitable. We must assume a posture of subjugation. This does not mean that we must completely surrender ourselves to the situation or give up our beliefs. Instead we must consciously take on a subordinate role and look for alternative means to achieve our ends. The Black Hole Card indicates that we must be indirect, diplomatic, possibly covert and certainly patient in our approach. If the Black Hole Card represents an individual that has power over us — for example, a superior in the work environment — then we must refrain from confronting them directly or aggressively. We must remain on good terms with the person and treat them diplomatically, acknowledging their power, while at the same time looking for more indirect means to achieve our ends or to escape their influence. This may seem duplicitous, but the Black Hole Card indicates that we cannot confront the person involved as an equal. We have no choice but to engage in indirect action, however unpalatable this may seem.

ACTIVITY: A RITUAL FOR SWALLOWING PRIDE

The kind of subjugation described by the Black Hole Card is very subtle. It involves swallowing our pride and relinquishing an idea of ourselves as a powerful, effective person while at the same time preserving our integrity. This is a difficult balance to achieve. It is important to let go of the anger, frustration and resentment we may feel at being stuck in this situation or our negative feelings about the individual who has power over us. Easier said than done, of course. We must 'swallow' a situation we find deeply troubling or unjust. The following ritual may help in this process. Bake a cake or pie that symbolizes the situation you are in. During the cooking process, consciously infuse the ingredients and the process with your intention to accept the situation and to relinquish your pride. As you eat what you have made, imagine that you are taking in the nature of the situation and are also absorbing the qualities that you need to deal with it. With every mouthful and swallow, intend that you are taking in the very essence of the situation and that your body is digesting the new abilities you will need. When you have finished eating, note down what these new qualities are. As the food digests within you, visualize these qualities becoming part of you.

GALAXY COLLISION
Keyword: Conflict

BACKGROUND: Sometimes galaxies are so close together that they are pulled towards each other by gravity. This mutual attraction causes distortions in the galaxies as they circle one another, resulting in long tails of dust and stars being pulled away. The immense forces generated by this encounter change the shape of both galaxies and stir up clouds of gas to create new cycles of star birth. Recent observations have led to a theory that this monumental encounter could create the kind of environment necessary for the development of quasars. This kind of stellar smash-up takes place in very slow motion, taking hundreds of millions of years. Eventually, one galaxy may totally swallow the other and so the whole process may regain a point of equilibrium.

INTERPRETATION: When two galaxies collide, both are affected by the process. The huge forces involved fundamentally alter the nature and the shape of both galaxies. The size of each galaxy means that

GALAXY COLLISION

they both generate large amounts of gravity. Even if one galaxy is much bigger than the other, both parties are irrevocably changed by the encounter.

If you draw the Galaxy Collision Card you may find yourself also on a collision course with another person or group. Although the collision of two galaxies is a physical event, the Galaxy Collision Card symbolizes collision on a more abstract level; the conflict that occurs in relationships between people. You may get drawn into conflict with another person for any number of reasons, but whatever the circumstances you will probably feel that the situation was in some way inevitable or unavoidable. It may be that the conflict is no-one's fault or you may feel convinced that you are right and the other person has erred against you. Irrespective of the circumstances, this conflict will be highly disturbing for both parties and, like the galaxies, both parties may be irrevocably changed. Although you may feel upset by the conflict, it is wise to remember that ultimately these encounters can be very creative and that they can clear the air between people. The conflict may release feelings that have been building up for a long time. In these circumstances it is better that the issue is out in the open. Try to approach the conflict as an opportunity for balance. No matter how convinced you are that you are in the right, try to accept that both sides must accept some responsibility for the conflict. Imagine you are the other person. What must they be feeling about the situation? Do not allow your personal sense of injury or aggrievement to cloud your judgement. While confrontation may be necessary in situations of conflict, try not to let things degenerate into point-scoring exchanges of insults where you may say things you do not mean and may later regret.

ACTIVITY: A PERSONAL EXERCISE IN CONFLICT RESOLUTION

In situations of conflict, it is beneficial to keep in mind an objective so that things do not deteriorate into a slanging match. Perhaps you feel that your point of view has not been heard by the other person. Or maybe you feel you have been let down in some way and you want to register your sense of betrayal. Whatever the circumstances, write down the origin of the conflict on a piece of paper. Identify the essential issue. Be honest, and try to seek out the real root of the problem. This may be different from the actual circumstances in which the conflict originated. Often the trigger for conflict is merely that — a trigger which ignites a much deeper and more important problem. Now write down what you would see as an ideal resolution to the conflict. Be fair about this — utter surrender and humiliation of your 'opponent' won't help either of you in the long run.

Once you feel you have a viable solution, make an effort to communicate with the other person. Tell them what you feel to be the origin of the conflict as diplomatically as possible. Ask them how they see the origin of the problem, which may be totally different to your idea of things. Then ask them to come up with what they think would be an ideal resolution. Arrange to meet and discuss your ideas. If both solutions can be accommodated, then you have a creative end to the conflict. If you are really not on speaking terms with the other person, you could try putting the above into a letter. For this to work, both parties must be committed to finding a resolution to the conflict. If you feel you cannot do this, or the other person does not respond to your overtures, then you may have to accept that the conflict cannot yet be fully resolved. Wait for a few weeks, then try to reopen the lines of communication. If the conflict is so severe that no resolution is possible, you may have to accept that the only resolution you are going to get is to let go of the relationship.

GALAXY CLUSTER
Keyword: Community

BACKGROUND: Incredibly, there are millions of galaxies in the universe, each with billions of stars. Like stars, these galaxies are not evenly distributed in space but tend to clump together to form clusters. Our own Milky Way is part of a galaxy cluster known as the Local Group, which contains more than thirty galaxies, including the Andromeda Galaxy and the Large Magellanic Cloud. Most galaxy clusters are so far away that only the largest are visible. One of these is the Virgo Cluster, which is fifty million light years away and contains over a thousand galaxies. Clusters themselves also group together with other clusters to form superclusters, containing millions of galaxies. Our Local Group, for example, is also part of a Local Supercluster. These superclusters are surrounded by immense voids which in turn dwarf the superclusters. The void around our Local Supercluster measures about 360 million light years. The staggering distances involved means that the light that reaches us from these distant clusters has crossed many millions of light years. The images we are actually seeing are of the galaxy clusters as they were millions or billions of years ago. The further away the clusters, the further back in time we are looking. Thus simply observing these distant galaxies can give us clues as to the history and origins of the universe.

INTERPRETATION: Most of the universe is made up of immense voids of space which contain — well — nothing! The void is broken up by clusters of galaxies. It is interesting that galaxies are not evenly distributed throughout the universe but that they cluster together, almost as if they were seeking companionship and comfort in the endless void. Humans also tend to group together, but we call our clusters communities and our superclusters society or culture.

The Galaxy Cluster Card represents the role of community in our lives. Whether we like it or not, we all exist within a community of some kind and we must follow the rules and conventions of this community. Ideally, a community offers support and nurturance to its members while laying down a set of rules or laws that they are expected to honour. However, people often feel constrained and restricted by the rules of their community and rebel against them. Many of us also feel that while we are expected to follow the rules, we do not feel accepted or acknowledged by our community.

In Western societies, traditional community structures have been irrevocably altered in the last few hundred years and many people feel alienated and cast adrift. On a more positive note, progressive models of community have been developed, where people who share a common cause or identity have gathered together. Whatever the nature of our own community, and however we feel about it, we must accept that we need communities. It is a basic human behaviour to gather together in this way. If the Galaxy Cluster Card appears, you are being asked to examine your feelings about your own community. What is your community? Do you feel a part of it, or do you see yourself as an outsider? It could be that you regard the people you work with as your community rather than your neighbours. Or do you feel you belong to an alternative grouping? Answering these questions will reveal your own personal attitudes to the idea of community. Try to focus on your feelings rather than getting sidetracked by the perceived shortcomings of your own community.

ACTIVITY: WRITING A MANIFESTO FOR YOUR IDEAL COMMUNITY

What is your ideal community? If you could define this community in any way, how would it look? Would the environment be urban or rural? What would the 'rules' be and how would the community support you? Write a short manifesto embodying the rules and values of your ideal community. Many great political thinkers began with this premise. They looked at the iniquities of their own society and developed a vision of an alternative, fairer community. The highly influential political movements of communism and socialism were born in this way, even if they did not fulfil the utopian visions of their creators. How might you introduce a flavour of your manifesto into your life? What contribution might you make to bring this about? How close to your ideal is it possible to get? Don't worry if this is not very close. This challenge has defeated the greatest thinkers of the last few centuries! Any positive benefit you can bring to your own life and to the lives of others is a rare and important achievement.

DISTANT GALAXIES
Keyword: Intuition

BACKGROUND: Some galaxy clusters are so large and so dense that they create an enormous gravitational field. Light rays passing through the gravity field are deflected, rather like a glass lens deflects and focuses light. Thus a distant galaxy cluster can act as a magnifying lens for the light from galaxies even more distant. This effect is called gravitational lensing and it enables us to see galaxies so distant that we would otherwise not be able to detect them. The gravitational lens distorts the light from the distant galaxies, making them appear thin and arc-like. In some cases, multiple images of the same galaxy are produced. Because of the huge distances involved, the light from these galaxies has been travelling to us for millions, or sometimes billions, of years. In studying these magnified galaxies we can therefore look back in time to see what they were like all those millions of years ago. The gravitational lens effect therefore enables us to see much earlier into the history of the universe than was previously possible.

DISTANT GALAXIES

INTERPRETATION: The gravitational lens effect means that we are able to perceive galaxies that we would not normally be able to see because of their immense distance from us. We gain knowledge of something that would normally be out of reach. In everyday life, most of us have had an experience of just knowing something that we really should not have known. For example, when the phone rings, we may intuitively know who it is on the other end. At the other end of the scale, some people claim to have fore-knowledge or precognition of important or disastrous events. It has been suggested that human beings have some kind of sixth sense which enables us to perceive things beyond our normal abilities.

The Distant Galaxies Card embodies this idea of being able to perceive what is beyond our normal capacity to know. Although such phenomena as ESP, telepathy or precognition are notoriously difficult to prove within the mainstream of the scientific method, most of us have some kind of personal experience of the inexplicable. All too often, however, these experiences come unbidden and the abilities that produce them seem out of our conscious control. If you draw the Distant Galaxies Card, you are being asked to develop your sixth sense or intuition in some way. How do you feel about your intuition? Do you respect your hunches or gut feelings or premonitions or do you try to explain them away with logic? The Distant

Galaxies Card is asking you to look at your attitude towards your own intuition. If you have not valued this ability in yourself, you may need to develop a more nurturing and respectful attitude.

ACTIVITY: DEVELOPING A RELATIONSHIP WITH YOUR INTUITION

Recall an occasion when you did not listen to your intuition and it turned out to be correct. Now recall another occasion when you did listen to your intuition and it was correct. Recall a third occasion where your intuition turned out to be wrong. Is there anything that links the three occasions? Was there any difference in quality in the time when your intuition was wrong? Were you being influenced by your own personal emotions or desires? Imagine your intuition is a separate person, sitting on a chair in front of you. What does it look like? What qualities does it have? Talk to it, make friends with it. Make an agreement with your intuition that you will try to listen to it more if it will promise to be truthful with you and not be unduly influenced by your own wishful thinking. Review your agreement at regular intervals by putting your intuition 'in the chair' and discussing your mutual progress.

DARK MATTER
Keyword: Mystery

BACKGROUND: If you add up the mass of all phenomena in the universe, the total only accounts for about 10 per cent of the actual mass of the universe. Where is the other 90 per cent? Astronomers have deduced that dark matter must exist to account for this missing 90 per cent, and indeed they have detected its gravitational effect upon visible phenomena such as galaxies. However, the nature of dark matter remains a mystery. Although it must have mass, because it has a gravitational influence on other objects, it does not emit or reflect light or other electromagnetic radiation. It could be that dark matter is made up of particles as yet unknown to us. Many such particles have been theorized but as yet remain undiscovered. Dark matter also has a crucial part to play in determining the origins and the eventual fate of the universe. We know that the universe is expanding and has been doing so since the Big Bang, but we don't know if it will always continue to do so. It has been theorized that, given enough dark matter, the universe may one day start to contract again and eventually collapse into a 'Big Crunch', reversing the process of the Big Bang. However, it now seems more likely that there is not enough matter in the universe for this to happen and that the universe will simply continue to expand forever.

INTERPRETATION: Although there are many theories about the nature of dark matter, nobody really knows what it is. Its true nature remains a mystery. There are things in life that we may understand to some extent, but an essential part of them also remains a mystery. The Dark Matter Card indicates an area of our lives that is mysterious. This could be a thing, a situation or a person. Try as we might, we cannot solve the enigma, even though we may think we know everything possible about the object of our inquiry.

When the Dark Matter Card appears, we are being challenged to accept that this area of our lives may always remain a mystery, that we may never get the answers. It may be that the answer does not exist or that it is being withheld from us by another. Or the nature of the situation makes it impossible for us to know. It can be very frustrating to be refused the answers like this and it can make us feel anxious and insecure. We can become suspicious and paranoid, obsessed with solving the mystery and finding the answers. While curiosity and determination are natural human responses to a mystery, with the Dark Matter Card it is essential that we relinquish the quest for answers and accept the mystery in our lives. In many cases, the answer to our inquiry cannot be given to us by an outside agency. We must discover it within ourselves.

ACTIVITY: CONTACTING MYSTERY

If we are presented with an insoluble mystery in our lives we have to find an inner resolution. We must accept that the reality of the situation may never be proved. The following exercise may help you with this process. Sit in a darkened room and close your eyes. Visualize yourself in a room which contains the answer to your mystery, but the room is so dark that you cannot see it. You are not allowed to turn on lights of any kind. You must use any or all of your other senses to discern the answer to your mystery. Take your time and make full use of all your other senses. Listen, touch, smell and intuit an answer to the mystery. Note down any impressions you get during this process, however bizarre or irrelevant. The answer may be given to you in symbolic form, in a similar way to a dream. Review your notes and try to make sense of the impressions you have received. It may help to do this with another person who knows the situation. They may give helpful and objective input, especially if your impressions are of a cryptic or symbolic nature.

THE UNIVERSE
Keyword: Completion

BACKGROUND: The universe is about fifteen billion years old and was created in a cataclysmic explosion known as the Big Bang. In the first few minutes of the Big Bang, particles were created and formed into atoms. Then forces such as gravity and electromagnetism came into being and all the matter in the universe was created. Many of these events took place in incredibly short periods of time — trillionths of a second after the Big Bang itself. Nobody knows why the Big Bang happened or what was there before it. However, we do know that the Big Bang originated with a singularity — a point that has no dimension in space but that is incredibly massive and dense. As singularities are also found in Black Holes, some cosmologists have theorized that Black Holes are in fact the 'originators' of universes, and that the Black Holes in our universe may lead to other universes.

INTERPRETATION: It is very difficult for the human mind to grasp the nature of the universe as a complete entity. While our minds can conceptualize about the nature of infinity it is much harder for us to grasp the true meaning of a universe that is infinite and yet is still expanding. Yet the end of our journey into the cosmos necessarily ends with the entire universe. This is as far as we can go, the point of completion. It is this concept of completion that is represented by the Universe Card. You have gone as far as it is possible to go with the object of your inquiry. A state of completion, of unity has been reached, even if you do not recognize it as such. You have reached the end of the road. However you may feel about the object of your inquiry, you must accept it as a finished entity. Sometimes we don't know when to stop with a project or a situation and we keep on trying to improve and change things even when the optimum point has been reached.

The Universe Card indicates that it is time to stop tinkering and accept that you already have the finished article, however imperfect you may feel it to be. The Universe Card sets a limit. It reminds us that we have travelled as far as it is possible to go at the present time. It is now time to return home to Earth and begin a new journey.

ACTIVITY: CELEBRATING COMPLETION

How good are you at recognizing when something is completed? Do you instinctively know and accept when it is time to stop or are you perpetually tinkering at the edges, unwilling to let things go? When you finish something, for example a creative project, a course of learning or simply paying off a debt, it is a good idea to formally recognize the moment of completion with a ritual celebration. We often do this instinctively with traditional celebrations such as graduation parties but it is equally important to celebrate the completion of more personal projects. This could take any form, from a quiet bottle of wine for ourselves to a full-scale party for our friends. Whatever the nature of the celebration, it is important that we reward ourselves for the completion of our project and acknowledge to ourselves that we have finally done it, that it is finally finished. We have reached journey's end at last and it is time to head for home.

THE FOUR FORCES: GRAVITY
Keyword: Love

BACKGROUND: We observe the effects of gravity every day, indeed we can feel its effect upon us every moment of our lives. It seems very familiar, almost mundane, but it is actually the most mysterious of all the forces. Gravity is a force of attraction that exists between every single particle in the universe. Gravity pulls things together and holds them in place; it is what keeps the planets in orbit around the sun and it stops us from floating off the surface of the Earth. It is the dominant force in the universe, working over immense distances and on enormous scales. Despite its importance, however, gravity is actually a very weak force. Although every single particle has a gravitational effect on every other, it is only on the large scale of planets, stars and galaxies that the effects of gravity become significant. It would be true to say that every human being has a gravitational effect on every other, but the size of this effect is negligible and we are totally unaware of it.

INTERPRETATION: We experience gravity every day, at every moment of our lives. It is so commonplace that we take it for granted and are usually oblivious to its existence. Yet gravity plays a crucial part in our lives. Its powers of attraction keep the Earth in its orbit around the sun and so make life on our planet possible. Yet gravity is also behind the extreme destructive power of a black hole, which pulls in and crushes anything that strays into its powerful gravitational field.

The Gravity Card symbolizes love, that much-maligned and abused human emotion, which is nevertheless such a crucial part of our lives. The positive effects of love are plain to see. Equally, the negative effects of lack of love are obvious, as are the destructive consequences when love is overshadowed by darker emotions such as possessiveness, jealousy and obsession. Like gravity, we all take love for granted and we are often a little embarrassed to admit the importance it has in our lives. Many of the world's religions hold love as their most cherished ideal, yet the practitioners of these religions often fall far short of this ideal. As do we all. Love is rather unfashionable at the moment and in our society we often equate it with sentimentality. This is a rather tragic state of affairs and the lack of love we have for those around us is evident in the continuing misery and hurt we inflict on each other in today's world. It is important that we not only love those close to us, but that we also love the world we live in; the precious Earth and all her children. The opposite of love is not hate, it is indifference. It may be the cynical indifference of good people as much as the violent actions of people filled with hate that threaten our future.

If the Gravity Card appears in a reading, you are being asked to examine your deepest assumptions about love. How do you behave towards those you love? Do you feel loved? With the Gravity Card, you are being asked to look at your whole life — past, present and future — not just at the current situation or object of your inquiry. Has your ability to love been changed or compromised through circumstance and experience? Have you closed your heart to others? The Gravity Card requires you to take courage and be more open-hearted, accepting both your own loving nature and the love that others have for you.

ACTIVITY: FINDING A PERSONAL SYMBOL OF LOVE

Take some quiet time to yourself and sit comfortably in a darkened room. Close your eyes and go inside yourself, with the intention of finding a symbol or an image that represents love for you. See this as a journey inside yourself. You could visualize an actual journey around your body, or a journey through a symbolic landscape. It may help to play a favourite piece of music. Take your time and don't worry if you can't 'see' anything; use your other senses to perceive the journey, such as hearing, smell, bodily sensation, etc. When you have found your symbol, focus on bringing it back into this world. 'Fix' the symbol in this world by drawing and colouring a picture of it. If the object you have retrieved is suitable, you might try to obtain it in reality — for example if your object is something like a cup or a mirror. Keep the object or the drawing you have made in a place where you will often see it as you go about your daily life. Reflect on why you have come up with this particular object, and what this means in your life. What does the image say about your own nature?

THE FOUR FORCES: ELECTROMAGNETISM

Keyword: Perception

BACKGROUND: The electromagnetic force gives us light and all other forms of electromagnetic radiation such as radio waves, gamma rays, x-rays, ultra-violet, etc. All phenomena in the universe (except the mysterious dark matter) give off some form of electromagnetic radiation. Electromagnetism operates at the subatomic level. Every charged particle is surrounded by an area of electromagnetism known as a field. This field is made up of subatomic particles known as photons. Photons have no mass but travel at the speed of light. When a particle or group of particles is excited, by being heated for example, energy is given off in the form of streams of photons. Photons thus act as transmitters of electromagnetic energy, which can be in the form of light, radio waves or any other kind of electromagnetic radiation.

INTERPRETATION: Electromagnetic radiation in the form of light enables us to see things in the universe. If the sun did not give off light, we would live in perpetual darkness. Other forms of the electromagnetic force such as radio waves, x-rays, gamma rays, microwave radiation, infra-red and ultraviolet allow us to perceive many objects in the universe that do not emit light. The Electromagnetism Card represents the many different types of perception available to us as human beings. The electromagnetic spectrum is a symbol of the wide spectrum of our perception, which includes not only our five senses but also our intuition (described by the Distant Galaxies Card). The totality of who we are is brought to bear in how we perceive the world. The weight of our experience and conditioning influences how we perceive things and our innate personality instinctively colours our outlook. It would not be an exaggeration to say that the world outside us is a mirror of who we are. We unconsciously select and edit what we perceive. We create meaning out of what is around us according to who we are and what we want to see.

If the Electromagnetism Card appears in your reading, you may need to thoroughly review how you perceive life in general. Look at your deepest assumptions about the world and honestly judge whether these assumptions are viable. Perhaps they have become like an old, comfortable suit of clothes — familiar, habitual but hopelessly out of date. Your perceptions may need to be challenged not just with regard to your current inquiry. This situation is probably a catalyst for you to overhaul your way of perceiving the world. You may be blinkered in your outlook and you could be missing something important through the narrowness of your vision. The Electromagnetism Card indicates that it is time for you to take off the blinkers and expand your idea of the world. Open your mind and remember the universe is a mysterious place and it may yet challenge many of our assumptions about its fundamental nature. Look at the history of humanity and see how many times the paradigm of how we understand our world has had to change. Usually these paradigm shifts are very uncomfortable and are met with much resistance. Remember, a few hundred years ago it was blindingly obvious to everyone that the Earth was flat and that if you travelled too far you would fall off the edge!

ACTIVITY: EXPANDING YOUR PERCEPTION
Close your eyes and imagine your perception is limited to your own body, your five senses. Absorb everything that you can feel, smell, hear, etc. Now imagine that your perception is expanding beyond your body. You can perceive what is going on in the rest of your house, in the street, in your town. Keep expanding your perception until you can take in the entire Earth. What do you experience? What can you sense? How do you feel? Now move outwards again,

into space, expanding through stars, nebulae, galaxies until your awareness takes in the entire universe. You are the entire universe. If you feel strange or get vertigo at this point, simply contract your awareness slowly back until you feel more comfortable, and then expand again more slowly. How does it feel to perceive the totality of the universe? Is it even possible? Can you put your perception into words or concepts that are understandable on an everyday level, or do you feel something beyond comprehension? Sense how much of the universe there is for us to understand and how little we really know of its true nature. Do you feel that the totality of who we are is reflected in the infinite universe? Or do you feel that the universe is a huge, lonely and frightening place? Remember the universe is a mirror; it reflects our natures back to us.

THE FOUR FORCES: THE STRONG FORCE

Keyword: Power

BACKGROUND: The strong force is the power source behind the atomic bomb and the creation of stars. As its name implies, it is immensely powerful. The strong force is the source of all nuclear reactions because it binds together the nucleus of the atom. The particles that make up this nucleus would simply repel each other and be split apart if it were not for the strong force. Nuclear reactions involve either splitting the atomic nucleus through fission or bonding the particles in the nucleus together through fusion. In both cases, the strong force is released with its immense capacity for creation and destruction.

INTERPRETATION: The strong force has an obvious power. There is no more powerful or destructive a sight than the unleashing of the strong force through an atomic explosion. The Strong Force Card symbolizes power, and the responsibility that goes with power. While the atomic bomb represents the negative use of power, there is a positive, balancing side to the equation. This is represented by the binding function of the strong force, which literally keeps matter together. The strong force is therefore crucial to the existence of the universe.

If the Strong Force Card appears, you are being asked to examine the way you handle power. This might be your own personal power or the power given to you in a work situation, a relationship or in any other area of your life. Whatever the circumstance, and even if you don't feel that you are in a position of power, the Strong Force Card indicates that your inner attitudes about your own power are being challenged at the moment. You must examine how you have used power in your life and what patterns of behaviour you have around power. It may be that you tend to feel powerless in the face of other, seemingly stronger personalities. Or by contrast you may have used your own mental or physical strength to impose yourself upon others, abusing the power you have over them. Think about your behaviour throughout your life. Do you feel you have learnt anything about how to handle power? Is it still a problem for you to accept power — or relinquish it? We are all powerful beings and the nature of our individual power is as varied as we are. The most powerful individuals are not necessarily those who are most obviously 'in power' in our society. Nor are they necessarily people who have a lot of money. Confusing wealth with power is a common error. Those that handle power best carry it lightly and subtly and do not impose themselves on others. Some of the most powerful individuals in history — like Gandhi, for example — believed in simplicity and humility, but the power of their message transcends any notion of political or economic power.

ACTIVITY: CONTACTING YOUR PERSONAL POWER

Close your eyes and take a few deep breaths and relax. Focus your attention on your abdomen. Imagine that inside your abdomen is a miniature sun, glowing with fire and energy. This sun is your power. Get a picture of it in your mind. What colours are associated with it? What does it feel like? Now ask your power some questions. Ask it what it wants. Ask it what it would like you to do. Ask it how you can use it in the world with responsibility. What is your relationship with your power; do you like each other, or is there a conflict? When you have completed this exercise, note down your impressions. In future, when you are in a situation where power is an issue, imagine your power glowing in your abdomen. Communicate with it about how to handle the situation. Ask it to help you, to advise you. Treat your power with respect and it will become your help and your guide.

THE FOUR FORCES: THE WEAK FORCE

Keyword: Evolution

BACKGROUND: The weak force operates in a much more subtle way than the cataclysmic strong force. It does not push or pull like the other forces, instead it is a force of change that operates over time — sometimes very long periods of time. The weak force works by converting neutrons in the nucleus of an atom into protons, electrons and neutrinos. This transmutation at the atomic level means that the weak force is intimately connected with the natural processes of decay. The weak force is put to practical use in carbon-14 dating, where the breakdown of carbon-14 atoms in decaying organic substances is known to occur in a very regular way. This enables archaeologists and forensic scientists to date human and other remains. The weak force can also be observed at work in the decay of radioactive substances and their gradual, slow loss of radioactivity over time.

INTERPRETATION
The weak force is a process that effects change over

time, exactly like the process of evolution. The weak force has a slow, gradual effect, like the formation of stalactites from dripping water. But its slowness and lack of dramatic effect does not mean that the weak force is somehow less powerful than the other three forces. We cannot see the process of evolution in our lives, but we know it has made us what we are. The Weak Force Card symbolizes this process of evolution, both in the biological sense and in the psychological sense of our own personal evolution.

If the Weak Force Card appears in a reading, you are required to take a long view, to observe how the process of evolution has shaped your life. In some ways, our evolution is beyond our conscious control. There is a biological imperative programmed into us that we have no way of altering. We cannot choose our gender, our physical appearance, the nature of our ageing process. We can only affect these things in fairly superficial ways, despite the advances of medicine and technology. We also have less control than we may believe over the shape and development of our lives. We may feel we have free will to make our own choices. However, there are moments in our lives where we feel we are driven by an invisible force which we hesitate to call fate. Whatever our religious beliefs and our attitudes about free will and fate, we have probably all felt that at some time or another, our lives are not fully within our own conscious control.

This is the mysterious inner process of evolution at work.

Although we do have many choices in our lives, we may ultimately have to learn that we must co-operate with the mystery within us. The Weak Force Card indicates that you are feeling the force of evolution at work in your life particularly strongly. You may be fighting against it and feeling resentful, powerless and victimized. Evolution can act on us in ways that are unpalatable and sometimes painful. It is hard to accept something without fully understanding it, especially if it is something that seems negative or destructive. This is one of the biggest challenges we face as human beings — to accept the process of evolution even when it seems unbearable and we can see no ultimate meaning in it. This paradox has exercised the minds of many philosophers and spiritual leaders throughout history. It is something we may never resolve in our lives. The best we can do is to co-operate with our own process of evolution and trust the universe which is our mirror and our avatar.

ACTIVITY: HONOURING THE PROCESS OF EVOLUTION

If you have access to a garden, choose a flower that is still in the process of budding. If you do not have a garden or it is winter, purchase some flowers, at least one of which is at the bud stage and place this flower individually in a vase. Each day, observe your chosen flower and see what changes have taken place. If possible, take a photograph of the flower every day. Observe its changing beauty at each stage of flowering. As the flower begins to wither and die, continue to observe it and contemplate this dying process as part of the natural process of the flower's evolution. Are you still prepared to find the flower beautiful as it dies? Can you see how its fading and dying serves to propagate the seed of the flower and so generate new life? Can you see the beauty in this process? Note your responses to each stage and see which parts you find the easiest to relate to, and which parts you find most difficult. If you have taken photographs, place them in chronological order and look at each one individually. Now look at the series of photographs as a whole, a single entity describing the life cycle of the flower. How does this change your perceptions? If possible, obtain some seeds or bulbs of your chosen flower and grow them in your garden or cultivate them in your house or flat. This will honour the continuing process of evolution within yourself by manifesting it in the world.

Thorsons
Directions for life

www.thorsons.com

The latest mind, body and spirit news

Exclusive author interviews

Read extracts from the latest books

Join in mind-expanding discussions

Win great prizes every week

Thorsons catalogue & ordering service

www.thorsons.com